PRAISE FOR BRAD CATON
AND *FIRST IN SNOW*

"Brad's pursuit of excellence is contagious. The insights and knowledge he shares will help everyone in our industry raise their game."

—**Kevin Speilman**, *customer experience officer, YETI Snow Management System*

"If you are a property owner, a property manager, or anyone who is associated with a property where it might snow, you need to read this book. The business of snow removal is not what most of us think it is. Brad Caton's book does an amazing job explaining the complexities of a service that most of us take for granted."

—**Jason Reid**, *builder of people, CEO Coaching International*

"Few people have a grasp of a topic as well as Brad does the snow business. He really is the Ice Man!"

—**Karl Burkat**, *CEO, Pinkbike*

"A wonderful and accurate depiction of the evolution and learning process of a seasoned and professional snowfighter."

—**Jim Anderson**, *snow operations manager, Premiere Landscape Services*

"An entrepreneur's compelling story of learning to conquer the elements and the industry. Brad is both human and inspirational as he shares his story and his wisdom in this book."

—**Corey Tisdale**, *cofounder, BBQGuys.com*

"*First in Snow* is a business story that reads like a *New York Times* best-selling novel. It's a raw and honest look at how entrepreneurial drive and innovation, coupled with work ethic and passion, are at the heart of being the industry's best in class!"

—**Anna Waltz**, *CEO and founder, MedEvoke*

"Just as Brad Caton elevated snow removal to a new art form he calls snowfighting, his book, *First in Snow*, elevates the entrepreneurial story to a truly gripping tale of adventure. That's because he has declared war on much more than just snow; Caton is passionately committed to creating a safe environment—literally—for his employees, his clients, and his clients' clients. If your business is frozen where it is, the Ice Man's book is sure to reignite your fire—and help you clear a path to next-level success through innovative thinking and over-the-top execution."

—**Denise Blasevick**, *CEO, The S3 Agency*

"Brad is an avid lifelong learner. This book will illustrate his methods and how learning from your customer, learning from experts, and learning from experience will make you the best in your field—and help you define it!"

—**Carol L. Clinton**, *MD*

FIRST IN SNOW

FIRST IN SNOW

INSIDE THE WORLD OF SNOWFIGHTING

BRAD "ICE MAN" CATON

Advantage®

Published by Advantage, Charleston, South Carolina.
Member of Advantage Media Group.

ADVANTAGE is a registered trademark, and the Advantage colophon is a trademark of Advantage Media Group, Inc.

Printed in the United States of America.

10 9 8 7 6 5 4 3 2 1

ISBN: 978-1-642250-37-4
LCCN: 2019917161

Cover design by Carly Blake.
Layout design by Megan Elger.

This publication is designed to provide accurate and authoritative information in regard to the subject matter covered. It is sold with the understanding that the publisher is not engaged in rendering legal, accounting, or other professional services. If legal advice or other expert assistance is required, the services of a competent professional person should be sought.

Advantage Media Group is proud to be a part of the Tree Neutral® program. Tree Neutral offsets the number of trees consumed in the production and printing of this book by taking proactive steps such as planting trees in direct proportion to the number of trees used to print books. To learn more about Tree Neutral, please visit **www.treeneutral.com**.

TreeNeutral

Advantage Media Group is a publisher of business, self-improvement, and professional development books and online learning. We help entrepreneurs, business leaders, and professionals share their Stories, Passion, and Knowledge to help others Learn & Grow. Do you have a manuscript or book idea that you would like us to consider for publishing? Please visit **advantagefamily.com** or call **1.866.775.1696**.

I would like to dedicate this book to the betterment of the snow and ice management industry and all of its customers.

CONTENTS

FOREWORD

When we formed the Accredited Snow Contractors Association (ASCA) in 2012, we did so with the mission of uniting the industry through the power of education and advocacy. Since then, we have had a number of legislative successes at the local, state, and federal levels of government and have seen our membership grow exponentially.

I learned early on that there were thousands of snow and ice business owners working quietly behind the scenes, content with running their business and focusing their energy solely on their local needs. Brad had been one of those people for a number of years after founding his Vancouver-based snow and ice management firm, Invictus. That all changed, though, when he began attending conferences and got serious about expanding his business. He joined the ASCA and quickly became a familiar face and voice at both our events and those outside of our organization, many of which I also frequent. The more Brad and I talked, the more I realized that we share the same vision and goals of improving our industry as a whole.

Brad is not in it for himself. He did not write this book to sell you a tool, a gimmick, or even himself. He wrote it to help our industry and those who depend on it. He wrote it to shed light on the actual work that snowfighters do, the challenges facing the snow and ice world, and the prevailing ideas on how we can solve them. Sure, like all business owners, he wants to improve his own company, but he sees the bigger picture, too. Every business is just one small piece in the industry puzzle. Brad knows that this puzzle's problems can only be solved by bringing all of the pieces together. Every snow and ice business's chances of growing and thriving long-term depends on the industry getting stronger and more organized. Brad understands that fact, and it's the main reason he decided to write this book.

This is one of the first books to be written about the snow and ice industry, and to say that it's needed or long-awaited would be a major understatement. The content of this book is a compilation of the kind of information and involvement that we at the ASCA have been hoping to see since we began our mission.

Our industry has seen a bit of peril over the past twenty years, resulting in great companies being unable to differentiate themselves very well. There has been an influx of companies undercutting services and selling themselves for less-than-profitable pricing. In the process, they have inadvertently taken value away from the industry. To make matters worse, lawsuits have also made a greater presence in our work, making it harder for the average company to maintain profitability.

Brad has always run a wonderful company, in the right way. Now he wants to give something back to the industry. He understands how to compete and succeed as an individual, but he also wants to ensure that our entire industry can do the same. A book like the one Brad has worked hard to produce is important to anyone and everyone connected to the work we do, mainly because most people don't understand the snow and ice management industry as a whole. Because the job we do is so often done when no one is around, our work is either unknown or misunderstood. In this book, Brad explains exactly what we do and why it's important, while detailing what we're up against if we hope to keep our work alive. I can't recommend this book enough. Read it, learn from it, and spread it.

Sincerely,

Kevin Gilbride, executive director, Accredited Snow Contractors Association

PREFACE

I'll come right out and say it: there are a lot of falsehoods about snow and ice management. Misconceptions abound when it comes to our industry regarding the costs, the professionalism, the training, and the bitter battle to stay insured that contractors currently find themselves in. For far too long, a curtain has existed between the industry and the customers it serves. Unethical practitioners and plenty of bad information have plagued the snow and ice business from the beginning, so it's not surprising that much of the public thinks every snow contractor is the same or that they can handle their snow and ice problems themselves rather than seek a professional snow contractor to do the job. In the eyes of many, after all, snow contractors are nothing more than wintertime yard people.

I want to change that. To prove it to you, how about we take everything you have been told about the snow and ice industry, tuck it someplace out of mind, and start over from the beginning?

In the chapters ahead, you will learn a brief history of the snow and ice management industry, the products and techniques we use, and what to look for in a good provider as well as receive a thorough lesson on some of the largest and most pressing problems facing our industry today. Along the way, I'll introduce you to a number of experts in the fields of technology, insurance, law, property management, snowfighting, salt manufacturing and distribution, and more. Combined, their insights and views provide a detailed, balanced, and critical evaluation of what the future may look like for the snow and ice management industry. So buckle up; it could be a bumpy ride.

CHAPTER ONE

THE SNOWFIGHTER

Flying is learning how to throw yourself at the ground and miss.

—DOUGLAS ADAMS

It began as a comedy. It was winter 2003, and for the last several years, I had been running my company, Invictus, as a modest-size janitorial company serving the Vancouver metropolitan area. Before that, I had worked in landscaping, so I felt I knew a lot about taking care of other people's properties. *What I can't do, I can figure out*, I thought. That was my reasoning anyway when my cousin, Shayne, a home builder and fellow jack-of-all-trades, suggested one weekend afternoon that we get into the snow removal business. My brow rose a bit. "Yeah? Why's that?" He shrugged. "Because a lot of my clients in the property management industry are in need of snow removal and deicing services. From what I hear, there just aren't many reliable ones around."

It sounded profitable to me, and a little exciting—a combination any young entrepreneur would find alluring. I had been a volunteer firefighter for several years and kind of missed the adrenaline rush of a call into danger to help relieve a disaster. Plowing snow and deicing a parking lot aren't quite the same as running into a burning building or cutting a car crash victim free from a mangled heap of steel and glass, but it's not office work either. I was in. "Let's do it," I told Shayne. He grinned and shook his head, and before we really knew it, Invictus was born.

We went to work making an inventory of our equipment later that night. It didn't take long, since between us we had two shovels, a pickup truck with a plow on the front, a garden tractor that didn't run, and my two-wheel-drive Mazda B2200 that, aside from snow tires, was, to put it mildly, ill equipped for snow-covered roads and parking lots. Nevertheless, determined to claim our fortunes as snow-fighters, we set off in search of our first job.

As it turned out, the search for a customer didn't take long either. I approached a client from my janitorial business the following day. She owned two industrial properties in the area, so I asked her if she had any interest in our new snow/ice removal package. To my surprise, she did. "Yes, absolutely! We are totally unhappy with our service provider, and we are looking for somebody new." *This might be easier than we imagined*, I thought.

The weather was terrible when she called. "Hey, Brad," she said. "There's an accumulation of snow on the site. There's a very small amount, but we'd like you to go in and plow it tonight just to be safe."

Temperatures had hovered just above freezing all day, but the snow/rain mix had begun to turn to ice as the daylight faded. It was 10:00 p.m. now, and I was still out finishing another job for my janitorial business. The day had been more difficult than most, but it wasn't entirely uncharacteristic either, given the time of year. It was mid-November in Western Canada. Icy conditions are normal for us, but I had a strange feeling that this wasn't going to be a quick-and-easy cleanup.

I hung up the phone and immediately called Shayne. At the time, he lived an hour and a half away, in a mountain town just east of Vancouver called Hope—an encouraging name, it would seem. "Hey, we have to go tonight," I told him. He sounded as though he had been halfway to a deep sleep. "Huh? What are you talking about?" he said, confused. "We have got to clear this snow on these parking lots, and we have to do it right now." Hardworking as always, he jumped into his truck without another question and began heading down the mountain to the highway. As he entered the highway, though, he blew a hose on his radiator and had to pull over on the side of the road. Of course, the rain was picking up now too, and a bit of snow was coming down with it. I finished the job I was on, and still, he had not arrived to pick me up. Finally, the phone rang, and Shayne told me about his trouble. I phoned the local BCAA (a roadside assistance organization in British Columbia) and tried to get a hose out to him on the highway, but to no avail. No one could get to him until the morning, so I drove out to him myself.

As my Mazda spun and crawled its way up the mountain, I remember glancing at the clock on the dashboard. In big red numbers it read: 1:00. Even if he fixed the problem by the time I got there, we would be lucky to start the job by 3:30 a.m.

To this day, I still don't know how we did it, but we made it back to Shayne's house at the top of the mountain in my truck. He took a radiator hose off an old truck in his driveway and prepared to drive back down the mountain. I remember walking out of his house behind him when I saw a small butane torch. I said, "Let's bring that." He looked at me like I had lost my mind. "What do you need that for?" he asked. "Who knows, man—I just got a feeling we might need it." I picked it up and slung it into the bed of my truck.

We got back to Shayne's truck on the highway, and as we prepared to replace the radiator hose, a Greyhound bus blew past us and grazed his plow. There was no damage to us, really, but the bus bent the shield and damaged the hydraulic arm on the plow. To add insult to injury, the bus kept going, splashing us with brown slush as it roared into the darkness.

We pulled the old radiator hose off and finagled the ill-fitting replacement back in place, putting the butane torch to use after all. By the time we hit the road, it was 4:00 a.m. People would be arriving at the job site in no time.

We got there at 5:00 a.m. and found half an inch of snow on the ground covering roughly fourteen acres of land we had to clear. Desperate, I said to Shayne, "Let's pull that tractor off and see if we can get it started." We climbed into the back of the truck and cranked up the tractor, and a gunshot went off. The thing kept backfiring, forcing us to abandon hope and leave it in the back of the truck.

We did a quick plow with the truck, and even with the dented shield and wobbly hydraulic arm, we were able to finish clearing the lot by 7:00 a.m. The client gave me a call the next day to thank me, and we knew we were in the snow business from that moment on.

With the money from that contract, I bought a plow for a Suburban I had and a little salter. The new equipment came just in time too, because we soon got hit with a foot of snow. Even with the new equipment, Shayne's truck, and a friend of his who joined our burgeoning operation, we couldn't keep up. We had three large sites, each more than twenty miles away from one another, and after plowing for three days straight, we were running on fumes.

Right when we thought we were getting on top of it, we would get hit with another snowstorm and have a foot of snow back on the sites. Plow trucks can't really remove the snow. They just push it into the corners. And after weeks of heavy snowfall, we had no more room left to push the snow. The lots were shrinking. I remember phoning the client, a client still to this day, and telling her, "Look, I have to apologize. We need some more equipment. I need your authority to get some Bobcats in here, or I have to walk away because I can't keep up." Thankfully, she gave us the authority to hire some contractors with Bobcats, and that was my introduction to loaders and skid-steer loaders—the backbone of most snow removal operations.

Like most entrepreneurs, I was learning as I went. A customer's request usually became my mission to solve one challenge after another, which ultimately led me to some other area of the business that I found to be more profitable, more efficient, or just plain easier. I remember a conversation with a customer during our second year in which they asked, "Do you know somebody that can do some salting for us?" I didn't know anyone in the salting business at the time. In fact, I didn't know anything about the salting business period, but one of the Bobcat contractors I had working for me did know a guy.

I gave him a call and asked if I could have a meeting with him to talk about salting. "Sure," he said.

The following year, I bought a salter, a loader, and a skid steer, and we did our own salting. It just started to grow from there. One thing led to another, and now the salting operation is one of our primary focuses.

Those were the early days of what would become Invictus Professional Snowfighters Ltd., a company now dedicated entirely to snow and ice management year round in the Pacific Northwest region of both Canada and the United States. But like so many in any industry can relate to, getting off the ground is a time when you're mostly flying by the seat of your pants and hoping you can figure out how to steer in time. If you can hang on long enough and make enough right decisions at a few key crossroads, you can succeed. Today, we have more than forty salt trucks on the road, with three hundred pieces of equipment out in a snowstorm and more than three hundred employees and contractors working. But as almost any snow and ice contractor will tell you, starting a business in this industry has never been easy. Unfortunately, it's poised to get even harder.

SNOWFIGHTING AT A GLANCE

Being a snowfighter is, in essence, about fighting winter storms and being as prepared as you possibly can be to do it properly. A job that is not done right leaves everyone frustrated. Imagine if someone piles snow in front of a garbage container or a fire hydrant, or maybe they're pushing snow into garden beds or drainage ditches, onto sidewalks or against parked cars. All such cases can lead to big problems for everyone.

In reality, we are a disaster relief service, but because we provide a mostly invisible service—with the majority of our work occurring late at night and early in the morning when people are sleeping—the average perception from the public sees us as Chuck in a Truck. You know, that guy who just strapped a plow to the front of an old truck and drives around at night for a few extra bucks. Plowing snow is easy, people think, and it can be. If the conditions are fair and the snow is light, it can be just that simple. But most of the time, the conditions are bad, and you work in dangerous circumstances until you are completely exhausted.

There is a massive amount of fatigue that occurs when you're in a storm and you're fighting it. It is one thing to fight snow for four to six hours. That's great. The average person works an eight-hour day, so you're beating the game, right? The challenge in the snow removal business, however, is that you never know when you will have a four-hour day or a sixteen-hour day. Mother Nature dictates your schedule, and she tends to do whatever she wants, regardless of whether you have had a day off this week. The type of snow the area receives, the depth of the snow, what the weather conditions are, and the temperature all play a massive role in how well the snow gets removed and how quickly.

The perception of most people today is that snow and ice management is a service similar to landscaping. The fact that many landscaping companies offer snow and ice management services to their customers during the winter months doesn't exactly help separate the two trades in the minds of the general public. Unfortunately, assuming that all landscaping companies can also handle snow and ice removal well couldn't be further from the truth. Snow and ice management is more akin to fighting a forest fire than it is to cutting grass, especially in a scenario in which ice is heavily present.

If you are not handling the conditions properly and being conscientious in your foresight and planning, you will get behind the problem quickly, and you may not be able to get yourself back on top of it. Presalting, anti-icing, monitoring weather patterns around the clock,

Snow and ice management is more akin to fighting a forest fire than it is to cutting grass, especially in a scenario in which ice is heavily present.

keeping your equipment well maintained, and staying prepared to go to work at any moment are all part of the job. What many people do not see are the things we do every day throughout the year to be ready for when a storm does come, ensuring that we are in the best position to take care of it at a moment's notice. People usually do not see that part of the business. Most see an expensive bill for clearing the ice and snow from their property, which they often feel has required an unnecessarily long time to do.

They're not wrong. It is an expensive service, and if you're doing it properly, it does take considerably longer to do the job than mowing your lawn in the summertime. Depending on the size of your service area and the amount of snow and ice your particular region receives, those costs add up quickly.

There are a couple of reasons for these costs. One is that the necessary equipment is quite expensive to purchase and even more expensive to maintain. The other reason is that you're working in the worst conditions for twelve to sixteen hours straight. As a result, you have to motivate the contractors who are risking their lives to do the work. And whether we like it or not, rarely does anything motivate people more than money, so the rate of pay for snowfighters is high. Not many guys want the job, and even fewer decide to stick with it after a season or two. You have to reward the ones who keep coming back and who do a good job; otherwise, you can't operate.

When I need to remind myself just how challenging this job can be, I think back to the first big snowstorm I ever faced in only our second year as a company. I didn't sleep for three days because we were fighting a terrible storm that year. I remember going to lunch with my wife at the end of those three days and sobbing at the table, bawling my head off because I couldn't handle it anymore.

That's the reality from a professional perspective. There's a big difference between your neighbor down the street who has a plow on his truck and will plow a few driveways for fifty bucks and the professional company that's taking on the legal and safety risks of ensuring that big sites like grocery stores, hospitals, shopping centers, and industrial workplaces are safe for people. To understand this dilemma and the impact it has on contractors and customers alike, you have to consider just how prevalent slip-and-fall claims due to negligence are in our industry. According to the Accredited Snow Contractors Association (ASCA), a whopping 83 percent of snow contractors have dealt with a slip-and-fall incident at some point. That's an incredible amount of risk levied on the contractor, and in some cases, on the property owner as well. You go from Pop Warner to the NFL pretty quickly in terms of contractor quality, and if you're willing to look closely enough, the differences in performance and results are just as noticeable.

CHAPTER TWO

SNOWFIGHTING IN ACTION

Never confuse motion with action.

—ERNEST HEMINGWAY

On March 11, 1993, a cyclone formed off the Texas coast at nearly the same time an artic high-pressure system began sweeping across the American Midwest and Great Plains. When the systems collided a day later, twenty-six US states and a large chunk of eastern Canada found themselves in the crosshairs of a wave of blizzards, tornadoes, whiteouts, and the ever-rare thunder snowstorm. The combination dumped several billion tons of snow and destroyed miles upon miles of land and property before dissipating three days later. In Mount LeConte, Tennessee, sixty-nine inches of snow collapsed roofs, trees, electrical lines, and dangerously strained bridges. Snowdrifts across portions of eastern North America rose as high as thirty-five feet and buried semitrucks, roads, and even homes. By the time it was over, the storm that would come to be known by such names as the "Great Blizzard of 1993," the "'93 Superstorm," and the "Storm of the Century" left in its wake more than $2 billion (roughly $3.4 billion today) in damages and an estimated 318 dead.

Snowfighters from throughout the United States and Canada came to help clean up the disaster, and while nothing could restore the lives lost, the lives of those trapped in cars and homes were saved in large part because of the tools, tactics, and resources of the snowfighter community. Tragic as it is, it's those times that people are able to see how truly important our industry is. But what is it, exactly? What do we actually *do* on the ground out there in the dark? It's a fair question.

THE SNOWFIGHTING TRADE

After a storm, it doesn't matter if the snow is heavy or light in terms of how we approach the initial cleanup. We use plows, blowers, shovels, and other tools and heavy equipment to pile and, in some cases, remove snow from areas in which it obstructs foot or vehicle traffic. Whether it's one inch or twenty inches of snow, our tactics don't change, though the types of equipment we use might.

If the storm consists of freezing rain or the snowfall itself brings ice with it, then we use a variety of anti-icing and deicing methods to secure the site. If there is a lot of precipitation in the air and the forecast predicts temperatures to drop, then we will prepare the site by heavily salting it. Salt's main purpose is to lower the freezing point of water, but it can also be used to melt ice that has already accumulated on surfaces. In other words, salt is our greatest weapon against ice in any form, as both a preventative and reactive tool.

Salt is our greatest weapon against ice in any form, as both a preventative and reactive tool.

There are, however, a few different ways that we use salt, depending on the temperature and the objective. To be exact, there are three main varieties of salts used for anti-icing and deicing. Sodium chloride, or rock salt, is perhaps the most common because it is effective, relatively inexpensive, and readily available. The problem with rock salt, however, is that it can reduce water's freezing point down to only about -5°F (-20°C). For conditions below -5°F, a salt blend is best. Magnesium chloride can prevent ice formation and melt ice in temperatures as low as -25°F (-31°C). Calcium chloride is effective down to -65°F (-54°C), but you're unlikely to ever face temperatures that extreme. If you see magnesium chloride or calcium chloride on an ingredients label, you can rest assured that the product covers extreme cold.

Salt is certainly an effective deicing agent, but unfortunately, it's hard on the environment. Salt eats away at metal and concrete, and it's harmful to grass, plants, waterways, and animals. There is a substance generally referred to as *ice melt* made from a compound called calcium magnesium acetate (CMA) that is supposedly safer for the environment. Be warned, though, that CMA is actually the same compound used to coat rock salt, so if your concern is the environment, be careful that you aren't just buying rock salt coated in CMA. If you do, once the coating melts off, you'll be left with regular old salt and the same problems it poses to the environment.

The Environmental Protection Agency has approved deicing products that use what are called *waste carbohydrates*, which supposedly help facilitate biodegradation. At Invictus, we developed our own line of deicing solutions known as EcoBrine. The base formula prevents freezing down to -21°F (-29°C) but is far less harsh on the property and surrounding environment.

Our "Premium" formula uses natural and safe ingredients that have effectively been used as ice melts for years, and its benefits to plant life serve as a bonus for environments high in vegetation. The CMA gives the mixture the strength to work effectively even at very low temperatures. It is a powerful deicer but is easy on the surrounding environment and surfaces, and it's harmless to children and pets. We also have a "Supreme" formula that's perfect for areas in which corrosion is a major concern, such as runways, bridges, ferries, drilling platforms, and transit platforms. This product is completely free of chloride and urea and meets all Leadership in Energy and Environmental Design standards. Reasonably effective and environmentally friendly as they are, most contractors use brines only about 20 percent of the time. That's because nothing has been proven to be as effective, durable, and cost efficient as salt, a topic I will discuss in far greater detail a little later.

THE GROUNDWORK: TECHNIQUES AND EQUIPMENT FOR GROUND CLEARING

When snow comes in, we take care of it right away. If we are in a cold spell and get a light, fluffy snow, and it continues to snow, we'll likely plow but will not put any deicing solutions down until the event is over. It's the size of the storm that makes a difference in how snowfighters respond, more so than what type of frozen moisture they are facing. For us, no matter what type of snow it is or how much of it we receive, we are still going to do five things: dispatch, scout, document, communicate, and decide on a course of action. At the end of the day, we have to be able to answer the question, "Is the site safe?" That's the most important priority in everything we do—the North Star, so to speak—of every decision we must make.

During a storm, we typically pile snow and spread out salt

to make sites safe nearly around the clock. In 2017, Vancouver received roughly twenty snowfalls in one season, a rare occurrence for a region accustomed to receiving no more than five. Seasons like that—while dangerous, exhausting, and certainly not ideal—help test our equipment, tactics, and team better than anything else can. You could say that we look for the silver lining whenever possible.

Our process ensures we have every parking stall and entrance-way cleared to allow everyone to show up and park at a business as they normally would. That's a main goal of ours, to make sure we keep good access and good egress for all walkways, parking areas, and handicap zones. Those are all priorities because it's important that our clients' business carries on as usual, without compromising safety.

We begin by sending a scout to the site, who reports back to us on the conditions of the site. For that report, we want to know what the snow and ice levels are and what obstacles there may be to our cleanup crew. We use that information to create a response strategy, which we then pass on to our own crew or to a subcontractor.

For a site without any snowfall, the first order of business is to lay down an anti-ice solution before the snow comes. Once the snow falls, we'll clear it, but the goal before that happens is to prevent the snow and ice from bonding to the cement. That's why we put down a layer of rock salt or EcoBrine first. Ideally, we won't have any bonding so that when we do clear the snow and ice, we are able to clear it more quickly and completely.

We have trucks to transport the salt and brine. We also have apparatuses (most commonly referred to as *spreaders*) specifically designed for dispensing salt and brine, which we typically keep on separate trucks. A plow truck is usually going to be stuck on a site for quite a while plowing, piling, and loading, whereas a salt truck moves from one site to the next as soon as it finishes its laps.

Sidewalks are the first thing that we clear. If we get a snowstorm, we dispatch all our sidewalk equipment first. That means the small gear—all-terrain vehicles, small tractors such as skid-steer loaders, snowblowers, and ground personnel—to get the sidewalks reopened as quickly as possible. Next, we focus on large areas, such as the parking lot and roadways. Depending on the level of snowfall, we will bring in box pushers, snow buckets, backhoe loaders, and all-wheel loaders to help get the job done. We want the site so safe that Grandma could walk on it in her high heels. That's the standard, and thanks in large part to advances in our equipment, it's a standard that is much easier to meet today than it was in decades past.

"The biggest thing in the last twenty years that has changed the efficiency market is box pushers," says Jason Case, owner and operator of one of the largest and most decorated snow and ice management companies in North America. Case Snow Management recently took home the number-five spot on the list of top one hundred snow and ice management companies in North America, as voted on by our industry, and earned a spot on *Inc.* magazine's list of the top five thousand fastest-growing companies in America. "The introduction of box pushers on front-end loaders dramatically changed the way people estimated snow and ice and built snow response plans and strategies. We're able to scale now. Instead of maybe two or three machines on a site, you need just one with a box pusher on it. That's created a lot of advantages in the market for people who were early adopters of that equipment technology. And it certainly changed the trajectory of what you were able to do in snow and ice, as far as performance goes. That one piece of equipment has changed the market tremendously."

Troy Clogg runs Troy Clogg Landscape Associates out of

Michigan, and with nearly forty years of experience in the snow and ice business, he's seen firsthand how far advances in equipment have come. Among the changes is the number of manufacturers who are dedicated to snow and ice management equipment.

"Back when we were first doing this, any heavy equipment we used literally was a road grader or loader with just a bucket," Troy recalls. "That would've been 1980s era. The snowplows were a 7½-foot straight blade with no rubber snow deflector, no wings, no nothing. Like most guys, we welded and made our own version of box pushers or containment blades over the years. We welded stuff to snowplows until you could buy parts for them. Fast forward, I'd say to the 1990s, and by 1992, we were exclusively using Boss Snowplow's V blades on any plow trucks. Then, five or six years ago, I moved everything to Douglas Dynamics and went with Western's Wide-Out [plow], which we love. Everything's now moved to Metal Pless's Live Edge and hydraulic wings, but we still use static box pushers, and all of our new stuff comes from Metal Pless."

With the right equipment in place, the job of a snowfighter is exponentially safer, easier, and more time efficient. But that doesn't mean you can overlook the techniques that are necessary to the job. Clearing should start at the building and move away from it, to the far end of the parking lot. When people come to the building, they're not concerned about being in the back of the parking lot farthest away from where they need to go. They're concerned about getting into the front door as quickly and safely as they can, so our primary focus is on the building's immediate surroundings and all the walkways and driveways where people are going to be walking and driving the most. Then we'll work from the building out to the far corners of the parking area.

Invictus uses a concept called "stay left," wherein crews come onto a property and go in a counterclockwise rotation around the building. We move from one area to the next, moving everything away from the building. If you have a big parking lot, such as a Walmart or a large shopping center, and you don't get to those outer parking areas until later that day or the next night, it's not the end of the world. If you don't clear the sidewalks in front of the store, that's the difference between people having access to the store or their place of work and not.

After we clear the traffic areas and, if necessary, salt, the crew cannot leave the site until it has been deemed safe by one of our inspectors. There are a number of items that inspectors check for before marking a site safe, but a few of the main things include clean piles, tight edges, and a full application of anti-icing and salt products. We also look at all the stairwells, walkways, parking stalls, entrances, egress areas, and building access areas to make sure they are cleared properly, free of large piles, and safe for pedestrian and vehicle traffic.

One of the most common problems that snow and ice management professionals see comes from people piling the snow on the high side of the property and not the low side. When that happens, the snow eventually melts and drains toward the low side of the property, freezing and melting over and over again as it does. That creates a very risky scenario, as thick sheets of black ice form and cover the ground. It's not tolerated on our sites. We make sure that everything is piled onto the property's lowest side. We try to ensure that those piles don't

One of the most common problems that snow and ice management professionals see comes from people piling the snow on the high side of the property and not the low side.

"bleed," but if they do, we place salt bags around them to make sure the water does not freeze and cause an unsafe area.

Once we have the snow and ice cleared from the trafficked areas, we then apply a heavy layer of salt or brine to make sure we deice any residual ice and also apply anti-icing to prevent new ice from forming.

FIRST IN CUSTOMER SERVICE

I've said it before, and I'll say it again. As with any service involving heavy equipment and great physical risk, hiring someone to handle your snow and ice problems is not cheap. It is also not something you want to wait to do until the very last minute. If a snowstorm is outside your door before you start searching for a professional, it is likely too late to snag a reputable professional with ample experience, equipment, and materials. We typically will not take on a new customer after August 31, a full sixty days before our winter season usually begins. Again, two months may sound like an excessively long time to scout a site and formulate a game plan, but we are not prepared to compromise the safety of our workers, our customers, our business reputation, or anyone else simply because we rushed our process for the sake of securing a new contract. It's just not sensible for any party involved. It takes time to assess the site; create a plan; clear the paperwork with all the parties involved (i.e., the customer, our insurances, our attorney, and any other parties with which the customer is legally obligated to); and ready the necessary materials, crew, and equipment.

We received a phone call late last November from a property manager in Portland, Oregon, who had found herself in the middle of a snowstorm. Caught off guard and desperate, she called me and said, "I noticed you guys do snow removal in our area. I have ten malls here covered in snow. Can you help me out?"

Rather than giving her an outright "no," I decided to explain our process and briefly educate her on our ASCA status and why we keep such a strict policy against taking last-minute jobs. "We are a professional company certified by the Accredited Snow Contractors Association. We organize all our jobs way ahead of time to ensure that our standards are not compromised. There's no way that I can come in and try to save the day when the chance of failing miserably is so high because I haven't had time to assess the site properly. It takes time to prepare. I'm not going to come in and help you this year, because that's not how we operate, and the risk is just too great. I'm sorry for that, but why don't I call you in June or July, and we can coordinate a strategy to manage all ten of your sites before the winter season starts? We'll come in and set you up early so you never have this problem again." The client agreed, and the following summer I booked all ten of her sites.

That's how we are educating the customer. We are saying no. More importantly, we are explaining why we have to say no—whether it's the insurance side of things, problems with the site itself, time and planning constraints, or something else—as opposed to always trying to say yes. I love saying yes, but on some things, you just can't afford the risk.

I truly enjoy our customers. I always have. And I have always wanted to help them with their pain points. Since we started Invictus, we've had to ponder many of the same questions: Why is snow removal so expensive? Why aren't there more people doing it? How come it's so difficult to find a good contractor to do this work? The financial cost I've discussed before owes mostly to high insurance premiums and pricey equipment and labor costs. As for the small number of snow removal businesses in our region, it just doesn't snow enough to support a large market. And the perceived poor quality of contractors? It's the nature of hard, seasonal, weather-based labor that's unpredictable and largely unregulated. But when we started to do the math and really understand the deicing and anti-icing model, that's when we knew where we could scale the business.

LEADING AN INDUSTRY

The idea of using salting techniques and innovative products to grow the business really grabbed ahold of me, because it's not something everyone else is doing. I really don't believe there is another person in all of Vancouver, British Columbia, that is thinking about winter and snow as much as I am. I think about it year round by attending snow and ice conferences and lectures, reading about developments in the industry, getting involved in snow and ice management organizations, and more. When there's a major weather event, many more are going to want the job, and every customer is going to want the job to be done right when they need it. But it's my goal to have it done correctly on every job site in every city in the Pacific Northwest, regardless of the severity of the conditions. To do that, I don't believe you can jump into it for a few months and then jump back out in the spring. I believe you have to stay committed to the trade around the clock all year long to become a true industry leader. We changed Invictus's model to meet that vision a number of years ago, and it's one of the primary reasons that we were able to scale as broadly as we have in our market within such a short amount of time.

INDUSTRY GAME CHANGER:
I believe you have to stay committed to the trade around

> the clock all year long to become a true industry leader. We changed Invictus's model to meet that vision a number of years ago, and it's one of the primary reasons that we were able to scale as broadly as we have in our market within such a short amount of time.

I'm a huge adventurer, so I do love the challenge and risk of such an ambition. I also believe that if you are not living on the edge, you are probably taking up too much space. This vision of having a large, systematic, and innovative company capable of leading the snow and ice management industry in the Pacific Northwest is a goal that lets me live on that edge in some respects.

To accomplish the feat of being an industry leader, we are changing the way we think about our job. Rather than snow and ice laborers, we aim to be snow and ice thought leaders. We obtained our International Organization for Standardization (ISO) certification to learn more about how we can do our work better as well as to show customers just how seriously we take our commitment to high-quality standards. In doing so, Invictus became the first and currently only ISO 9001/SN 9001 certified snow and ice company in the entire Pacific Northwest region. What is an ISO certification? A brief history of the certificate is in order.

Rather than snow and ice laborers, we aim to be snow and ice thought leaders.

The ISO is a standards organization that formed right after World War II, as an accrediting body to certify that people who were manufacturing parts for the airlines, or for the airplane business in general, would all conform to a set of manufacturing standards. The idea was that parts that were manufactured in, say, Canada, Japan, Germany, or France would be interchangeable with parts made somewhere else. Parts for one type of engine, for example, would be the same regardless of where they were manufactured.

That concept took hold, and even today, you might see a manufacturing company with its sign out front that says ISO 9001. An ISO 9001 company means that it is certified by ISO and that it is following procedures that are generally accepted as standards across the globe.

In recent years, ISO certification has branched out into service companies. An ISO certification means that you have a set of processes and procedures in place to fix things that go wrong and that are published, repeatable, and followed consistently.

Invictus is different because we operate to the highest industry standards on every job, and the main reason for that is because we are the only company in our market that's focused on snow and ice all year long. We never stop researching and trying out new techniques, tools, technologies, and strategies relative to snow and ice management. We simply could not do that if we spent the better part of the year working in other trades.

We have also brought in the best equipment for the job. That's the competitive advantage that we are going after. Our EcoBrine system has especially lifted our reputation as a leader in snow and ice innovation up to new heights.

Large retail chains and industrial companies have had so many slip and falls and have had such a bad experience with underperforming operators that they have grown skeptical of, if not disillusioned with, the snow and ice business as a whole. We want to change that, and so far, it's working. We are able to prove to these types of clients that the industry is progressing, that it is trustworthy and capable, and that it is incredibly important to both their bottom line and to public safety. It's not too difficult for a business in our industry to earn trust, really. Just stick to the truth and make sure that you're delivering what you said you would deliver. It's that simple. I would rather underpromise and overdeliver for our customers to build and maintain a reputation for being an exceptional company. For 99.9 percent of the clients we work with, we are that company.

CHAPTER THREE
INVICTUS: WHAT WE DO

The snow doesn't give a soft white damn whom it touches.

—E. E. CUMMINGS

With Invictus up and running, I spent the first few years raising clients and learning the ropes of running a growing company day to day. Nothing about those early years was easy, but we survived, and slowly but surely, we began to thrive. I wanted to learn as much as I could about this industry, so I set out to talk to as many experts as I could—the people who had been doing it for years or even decades longer than I had.

My goal was not just to run a business but to become an industry leader, someone who could find or create new innovations and methods that could help other snowfighters improve and excel in their own operations. I knew that the continued growth and success of my business depended on keeping myself on the forefront of industry trends and developments. I joined associations, attended conferences year round, and spent months interviewing a wide array of experts connected to the snow and ice management industry—from property management firms to attorneys and advocates to insurance agencies to other snowfighting entrepreneurs like myself—to learn as much as I could about what these trends and developments looked like and the impact they either had or would have on our industry.

Like most successful companies, Invictus places a great deal of importance on culture, which makes a difference for the people you work with and for. Want a trusted snowfighting company? Take its culture into consideration. How does it operate? How does management treat their employees and subcontractors? How do their employees and subcontractors treat management, and how do they approach their work? Do they behave professionally? Are they using current methods? Are they taking proper precautions and documenting their work? These are all visible signs to the customer that provide reliable hints at how the company runs its business behind the scenes.

THE INDUSTRY PROFILE

To fully understand what a snowfighter does, it helps to first know a little about the industry as a whole. A look at the numbers will help to create a more thorough profile.

In North America alone, roughly 35,000 contractors operate in the snow and ice industry, and they in turn employ more than 400,000 people during the winter months. Depending on winter snowfall totals, it is an $8 billion to $10 billion industry. The industry's leading association, the aforementioned ASCA, estimates that the average snow contractor brings home around $542,000 of seasonal snow revenue and employs seven year-round workers; three year-round, part-time workers; twelve seasonal workers; and ten subcontracting companies. Of those subcontracting companies, the average employee rate ranges from one to thirty employees, depending on the season and the size of the market.

Sixty-seven percent of snow contractors also run a landscaping business during the spring and summer months. The remaining 33 percent comprise allied segments of the service industry (e.g., excavating, general construction, and paving), in which annual revenue is often heavily affected by winter conditions. In other words, the snow and ice management industry is not just good business for the small number of professional snowfighters who focus their efforts on snow and ice year round. This industry is the primary employer for hundreds of thousands of people throughout the winter and for thousands of subcontractors—often small business owners from other professions—who assist in executing the work. As a whole, the industry relies on people willing to work long hours in some of the most dangerous conditions during busy holiday seasons to make society safer.

> **The industry relies on people willing to work long hours in some of the most dangerous conditions during busy holiday seasons to make society safer.**

In my years of learning as much as I can about the snowfighting industry, I've met experts in different corners who understand the industry landscape and trends.

One such expert with decades of firsthand experience is Jim Anderson, who serves as the snow operations manager for Premiere Landscape Services, a large landscape design and construction firm based in Michigan. Jim is a great example of the seasoned snowfighter, from his beginnings in the industry to his passion for the trade itself.

"I was born and raised in snow country, if you will," Jim

explains, "but then during the late seventies, I went down to Florida and worked for a large landscape contractor there. Of course, there's no snow down there, so I learned a lot about landscape construction and irrigation. I came back home in the late eighties and got involved with a property management company. In the wintertime, of course, you do snow management and snow removal. And that was my first year doing it, probably in '89, when I got back [to Michigan]."

Jim describes his experience in the industry during those early years as akin to exploring a wild frontier, a description he attributes to how fragmented the industry was and how few standards existed at the time, especially compared to the movement we see today to bring about more industry-wide standards and training certifications.

"It wasn't like it is now," Jim says. "People just kind of did it back then. You could make your own rules, do your own thing. You also could do it on the side. You could do other things and work at night. It was really something landscapers did in the wintertime because they already had the connections. There weren't any standards. Nobody really trained anybody. You just got in the truck and [plowed]. Now, there are a lot of great standards. There's a lot of information out there on things that you should be doing."

When it comes to which era is easiest for a contractor or entrepreneur to operate in, the 1980s and 1990s or today, Jim says there are a lot of pros and cons to each side of the coin, but ultimately, he believes the industry is harder to break into today than ever before.

"You didn't have restrictions back then, and the expectation wasn't as high as it now. Maybe it was easier back then, because the expectation was more realistic. Nowadays it's very litigious. We did a lot of stuff without contracts back then, but now you don't do anything without a contract. There didn't seem to be that much risk and liability before. People weren't suing everybody at the drop of a hat. Now it's a big deal."

That "big deal" has left business owners with a marathon of paperwork to endure. On top of employee and subcontractor training, a professional snowfighter must engage in complex, significantly time-consuming documentation procedures to satisfy protections from legal claims. As people have become more inclined to pursue litigation over slip-and-fall cases in recent decades, the snow and ice industry turned to detailed weather reports and thorough, documented site inspections—which outline where to place snow, where site drainage occurs, where hazards are, hours the property is open to the public, and preexisting property damage. These records are kept for every snow and ice event, and their recording begins as soon as the crew clocks in to the property. Afterward, the crew documents every service they performed, what services were not performed and why, and the time they exited the property.

This documentation helps to protect snow contractors, but even those measures are not impenetrable in a court of law. Even the most frivolous and bogus slip-and-fall claims have managed to pierce holes in these documentation practices to win the case for the plaintiff. In fact, snow and ice related lawsuits account for a significant share of all liability claims against small businesses, with water and freezing damage accounting for 15 percent of all claims, and slip and falls comprising 10 percent of all claims.[1]

With all the precautions in place, you may be wondering why snow and ice contractors so often find themselves in some form of litigation. The best answer I can point you to is the contract. Most contractual agreements that contractors sign with the property

---

1   "10 Most Common and Costliest Small Business Claims," *Insurance Journal*, April 9, 2015, https://www.insurancejournal.com/news/national/2015/04/09/363801.htm.

owner or manager assign liability to the snow contractor. Given that many snow contractors are only part-time snowfighters, they often unknowingly, or reluctantly, accept poor terms for the sake of securing the contract. There was a time when Invictus accepted bad terms in contracts as well, but as we gained experience and learned just how devastating a bad contract can be, we no longer accept contracts that give property owners and managers more control over our work than we have. The same can be said for Jim and his team.

"That's not our problem," says Jim. "I look for that stuff. I think, for the most part, people sign contracts and get involved with things that they really have no business getting involved with because they're just trying to get to work. They may think, 'Well, they can't change a contract. It's a contract. I have to sign it if I want to do the work.' Which is not true. You don't have to do that."

Additionally, in a highly competitive market, you can always find contractors willing to work for the lowest dollar, regardless of the liability risks involved. The most unfortunate thing is that for property owners and managers, their tenants, customers, and anyone else connected to the property, inexperienced or just outright irresponsible contractors are usually incapable of running a successful snow and ice removal operation, much less safeguarding themselves from the slip-and-fall litigations that plague the industry.

THE SNOWFIGHTER'S JOB

Snowfighters are, for the most part, a nocturnal breed. Our season in southwestern Canada usually begins on Halloween, perhaps the perfect holiday to say farewell to the sunshine for a while. For others in North America, the season starts sooner, and for some, it starts weeks or even months later. We all, however, begin our season when the days are the least hospitable to people. That means the job of a snowfighter demands certain characteristics from a person.

Jason Case is a third-generation snowfighter who now runs one of the largest snow removal fleets in the country through his own outfit, Case Snow Management. Jason's company employs between eight hundred and one thousand people during the winter season and approximately fifty throughout the rest of the year. Case Snow Management has been ranked fifth in the list of top one hundred North American snow and ice management companies by *Snow Magazine*, and Jason himself was named Snow and Ice Management Association's (SIMA) CEO of the Year in 2017. Case Snow Management is also a seven-time Safety Award winner and a three-time recipient of SIMA's Excellence in Snow and Business Award. It's safe to say that Jason knows this business and what it takes to succeed in it better than just about anyone. He also knows what it demands from the individual.

When asked what type of personality a typical snowfighter must have, Jason is quick to make an important distinction. "There's a certain underlying characteristic an individual might possess to be in the snow and ice business. You get an array of personalities, but a characteristic would be work ethic. The ability to endure long hours, high-stress environments, and still have the ability to roll up their sleeves and fight in a snow emergency response situation that's unpredictable in nature demands a different characteristic than if you're a banker working nine-to-five hours. These guys have a lot of determination. They're also business owners. I have a lot of guys who have a great mix of blue-collar and white-collar abilities, meaning very hands-on and possess tradesman skills to work in the field, but who also understand what it takes to be in business from the insurance side of things. They understand cash flow management, banking, managing an organization, payroll, etc."

Despite the range of personalities among snowfighters and the diversity of characteristics and skills needed to do the job well, the basic demands of the actual work are the same for everyone. A snowfighter's day typically begins between eight and ten o'clock at night, with the preparation of equipment and supplies, and doesn't end until the last of their cleaning routes are finished, usually around five o'clock in the morning. You wake up when the sun is going down, and you lie down when the sun is coming up—that's the life of every snowfighter during the winter season.

You wake up when the sun is going down, and you lie down when the sun is coming up—that's the life of every snowfighter during the winter season.

While some companies employ a two- or three-inch minimum before activating a team, Invictus goes by a zero-tolerance policy for snow and ice because most of our sites are high-traffic sites (i.e., shopping malls, grocery stores, hospitals, and business centers). That means we stay busy nearly every night during the winter, and the hours and conditions can exhaust an inexperienced person well before the season ends.

One of the biggest challenges for Invictus (and I'm sure for every other snow and ice removal company of our size too) is making sure we can assemble a large enough team for any kind of weather event, whenever we need them. What we do as a profession is a tough and dangerous job, and naturally a lot of people will fall away from it after a single season—or even a single day. Virtually all of them are attracted to the money, but as they say, money isn't everything. At the end of the day, a contractor might make a couple of grand, but you would be surprised how many would prefer to stay in a warm bed and sleep than make that much money trudging around in a snowstorm all night. At Invictus, we are constantly working to build a rapport with the contractors that we work with for that specific reason. We can't just call them up in the middle of the night in November, after not speaking to them since March. We have to build and maintain relationships with them all year long.

For Invictus, our biggest focus is on training our workers when they're not working. We have to get in and train every contractor for an event that may or may not happen. That can be a difficult task, and in the beginning, it was akin to herding cats. It's not too difficult to learn how to operate and handle a snowplow, loader, salter, deicing solutions, and the rest of our equipment and tools. It's also not that challenging to learn the basics of proper snow and ice removal. Like so many other professions, however, it is difficult to keep people engaged day in and day out, even if they are earning significantly more than most service management jobs. To combat the tendency to burn out or be lured away by year-round work, Invictus has worked to establish a business concept in which every contractor can earn well seasonally while also feeling like an integral part of the team year round through training programs, company events, routine communication, and off-season work opportunities.

INDUSTRY GAME CHANGER

To combat the tendency to burn out or be lured away by year-round work, Invictus has worked to establish a business concept in which every contractor can earn well seasonally while also feeling like an integral part of the team year round through training programs, company events, routine communication, and off-season work opportunities.

Since Jason founded Case Snow Management, he's worked to accomplish the same kind of consistency with his crew as we have at Invictus, and a big part of how he achieves that is simply by ensuring they have enough work to stay busy. An abundance of work is not an entirely easy way to keep a team fully staffed year round, which is why Jason looks for a key motivation from his workers: a willingness, and even desire, to work hard.

"I'm not sure what the motivation is for the majority of snow and ice contractors throughout the United States," Jason explains. "Certainly our motivation when we started this organization was built on just rolling up your sleeves and working hard and getting it done through the wintertime and then having the ability to breathe when the springtime came around. And not have to transition immediately into landscape or pavement or construction of another line of business.

"Through my lens, we are the only true snow and ice company in that top five that has the amount of equipment, man power, training programs, boots on the ground, [and] resources to perform snow and ice services not to just sub out work. We are more of a hybrid model organization. Perhaps that was a catalyst to our growth where we don't just bid jobs, get the contracts, and then hire a service provider to fulfill the obligations of those contracts and kind of walk away. We are in the field with them. We are meeting them face to face. We are sending our fleet of equipment to support them. We provide training programs to those service providers because they are day-to-day guys in business, and their turnover is just as high as anyone else's. We are a good resource of business for them, and we want them to grow with us. But that's the difference between a national company that just subs out work versus Case Snow Management, which has two divisions. We have a self-performing division, and we also have a national division that works with service providers, but we overlay that with dozens and dozens of field managers that go out there and shake hands with our customers and shake hands with our partners."

THE INDUSTRY'S HIGHEST STANDARDS

Detailed oversight, training, and physical engagement on site is essential to running a quality operation in this business. As I said earlier, snow removal is similar to firefighting. We work with heavy equipment in dangerous conditions around the clock. One main difference, however, is that we have no way of closing off a scene to better ensure the safety of ourselves and those around us. We might have children running around the site as we work to make it safe or an elderly woman pushing her cart right next to us. As long as the site is unsecure, we cannot do our job to the best of our ability. In my opinion, a site should be shut down while we work to make it safe for pedestrian and vehicle traffic. That rarely, if ever, happens. If you own a grocery store, a mall, a factory, a bank, or some other business, your success largely depends on the ability of customers and workers to get into and out of the property. If they can't, then you lose money. I get that, but both the property owner and the snow removal company stand to lose much more if someone slips and falls or gets injured by a piece of equipment because the site wasn't clear before opening it up to traffic.

One way we are combating that problem is by creating ways to establish industry-wide quality and training standards. In 1947, the ISO pooled a group of national standards experts from more than 160 countries from all over the world to create the ISO 9001 certification. After an applying company, its staff, and contractors complete a training course and prove that they have met the ISO's requirements, that company becomes a certified member of the ISO network, a distinction that lends credibility to a company's high safety and quality standards. ISO also requires members to renew their certifications on a regular basis (usually every three years) to ensure that each of its members stays up to date on their quality management standards.

Fortunately for Invictus, keeping a current ISO certification has helped us earn and maintain favorable views from insurance companies. They know we take what we do seriously and that we do everything we can to provide the most competent and highest quality service that our industry has to offer. We follow the standards set by the ISO 9001 manual, which covers the service management sector and breaks the standards down into five categories, as follows:[2]

- Requirements for a quality management system, including documenting information, planning, and determining process interactions

- Responsibilities of management

- Management of resources, including human resources and an organization's work environment

- Product realization, including the steps from design to delivery

- Measurement, analysis, and improvement of the quality management systems through activities like internal audits and corrective and preventive action

As Jim mentioned, it's very common to see what I would describe as part-time professionals in the snow and ice management

---

2   The manual can be found at the American Society for Quality website: http://asq. org/learn-about-quality/iso-9000/iso-9001-2015/.

industry. These are companies or individuals who perhaps run a landscaping company or a construction business but opt to do snow and ice removal in the winter when their regular work slows down. The problem is that they typically aren't as committed to learning the newest and best techniques in the field, nor are they investing fully in their snow and ice removal equipment and training. It's a seasonal gig for some extra cash until they can get back to their "real" job. I'm not knocking those guys; I used to be one of them. But if our industry is going to improve its insurance problem, it will begin with accreditation. Once the image of our industry is seen as one of serious, well-trained professionals whose work saves lives, we have a better chance of elevating the profession as a whole as well as the public's perception of the importance of our work. Standardizing our processes and requiring only accredited snow and ice contractors to be on a site will ultimately provide better protections for snowfighters and property owners at once, all while ensuring that we can do our jobs as safely and effectively as possible.

CHAPTER FOUR

THE LEGAL SIDE: PROTECTING AND DEFENDING THE WORK WE DO

Quality means doing it right when no one is looking.

—HENRY FORD

Josh Ferguson, a leading attorney in the snow and ice management sector, leads a team covering slip, trip, and fall cases in the US states of Pennsylvania, New York, New Jersey, and Maryland. Day in and day out, Josh and his four associates represent contractors and property owners alike in cases that could potentially cost their clients millions. He estimates that roughly 60 percent of his cases are representation of snow and ice management contractors against slip-and-fall claims. He spent the last fifteen years litigating hundreds of these types of cases and currently serves as outside counsel for the ASCA.

In his role as outside counsel, Josh was on the team to review the organization's current industry standards before they came out. He also drafted several of the ASCA's education classes. If a contractor goes to the ASCA to get certified, they will take a couple of classes that Josh created. He was also heavily involved in drafting some model legislation for the organization, including an anti-indemnity bill that has now been passed in two states. Josh even testifies regularly in court cases regarding the state of the industry, especially when the questions pertain to that bill specifically. In short, Josh knows his stuff, and according to him, two of the biggest threats to the job are the waning of insurance carriers willing to insure contractors and an increase in slip-and-fall claims.

Two of the biggest threats to the job are the waning of insurance carriers willing to insure contractors and an increase in slip-and-fall claims.

"We are seeing a rise of [contractors] having their claims denied for lack of insurance or exclusions on their policies," Josh says. "I would not pin it on one thing ... but slip-and-fall claims have certainly increased. Historically speaking, a plaintiff's firm, [a slip-and-fall claim] was not their top priority, especially the volume firms. They would rather run with a product liability or a motor vehicle accident claim because they are sound. The slip-and-fall claims on ice are a little bit tougher to prosecute. There was certainly a change on that, and I think part of it was when they realized that, as soon as they present the claim, most of these snow contractors did not have any kind of documentation to show what they did. [Plaintiffs' firms] found that they were winning them. That was certainly part of the reason [for an increase in claims]."

But Josh is quick to point out that these problems also stem from the huge increase in marketing dollars that plaintiffs' firms have put into TV commercials, billboards, and other marketing materials. When was the last time you saw a cheesy commercial or a billboard advertising an attorney's ability to sue someone? I bet it wasn't more than a few days ago. Educating the public that those types of claims are worth a lot of money and that they should file them has, according to Josh, contributed to the increase in litigation that contractors and property owners are currently facing. "I think there is a public awareness that was not there before, that now if you slipped and fell in a parking lot, you have a lawsuit. I think it came from multiple reasons."

Another of those reasons, albeit one that is arguably smaller in effect, stems from a change in federal law that came about during the 1990s, which asserted that a judge did not have to sanction lawyers for bringing forward frivolous lawsuits. That bill was challenged in 2013 with the passage of the Lawsuit Abuse Reduction Act, which requires courts to fine a plaintiff if their lawsuit is proven frivolous.[3]

"When they changed the rules of the federal procedure, to make it discretionary for judges to sanction plaintiffs' attorney[s] to file frivolous lawsuits, that certainly had some level of impact on the plaintiff's bar taking the riskier cases knowing that their risk was not having to pay back on the other side if it turned out to be a claim that didn't have a whole lot of merit," says Josh. "I don't think that was the number-one or -two thing, but I think it was one of many things that started to turn at the same time."

Of course, these cases, frivolous or otherwise, don't present themselves. Someone has to have an accident, whether it's a car accident or a slip and fall, and actually call a plaintiff's firm.

---

3   Pete Kasperowicz, "House Approves Automatic Fines for Frivolous Lawsuits," *The Hill*, November 14, 2013, https://thehill.com/blogs/floor-action/votes/190310-house-approves-automatic-fines-for-filing-frivolous-lawsuits.

"I think that marketing was number one, and then some of the other things fall into place," Josh explains. "The change in the rules of procedures certainly impacted it. Maybe the biggest part of it was that (plaintiffs' firms) were spending dollars to educate the public that these are claims in which they can recover from."

Plaintiffs' firms and the public also learned that snow and ice contractors often weren't documenting their work very well, making them even more vulnerable to potential legal claims against them. Another piece to this puzzle is the contracts between property owners and contractors, with specific respect to liability.

According to Josh, the contract language relating to defense and indemnity provisions is perhaps the biggest issue when it comes to litigation threats. When a property owner or property manager controls when and how a property can be serviced but still pushes their indemnity down to the contractor, there is a breakdown in trust between the two parties as well as a serious, and potentially fatal, financial risk to the contractor's business.

When a property owner or property manager controls when and how a property can be serviced but still pushes their indemnity down to the contractor, there is a breakdown in trust between the two parties.

We at Invictus have plenty of experience with bad contracts because we used to accept nearly any and all terms in the early days before we knew better. And even when we did know better, we still sometimes accepted them in an effort to grow the company at all costs. I think most contractors new to the industry will tell you the same thing. Jim Anderson is one of them. I asked Jim for his thoughts on client-contractor contracts and what he thinks could be done to improve the terms as well as the relationship between property owners and managers and contractors.

He paused for no longer than a second before he replied, "Better indemnification language. By that I mean not making us liable for every little thing."

Jim also explains that there's often a breakdown in communication between clients and contractors, mostly because few clients understand what they're asking a contractor to do to reach their expectations. We all get a little suspicious when we are paying someone a lot of money to do a job that we can't readily see them doing, and that contributes to these fundamental misunderstandings of what is possible when trying to remove snow and ice from a site during a weather event.

"We can service a site easily three to four times in a day when it's open," explains Jim. "But we are not going to stay inside all the time. If you have a two-inch spec [a contract stipulation requiring a contractor to plow the site once two inches of snow accumulates on the site], yet you want it black and wet all the time, well, the spec is contradictory to itself. I can't salt delay an inch of snow in the middle of winter with the ground frozen and the air temperature at 20°. I have to plow that away. You can't salt it away. If [a contract] tries to trick you into specs, like a two-inch trigger, but in the next breath wants 'zero tolerance,' if you will, it's just not realistic for us to do."

A lot of the bad contract terms are due to property owners or managers wanting to dictate the terms in which a contractor can come and service a site. That's understandable, of course. A business owner doesn't want anyone interfering with their ability to conduct business, and a snowplow driving around in your parking lot during operating hours may do just that. But not only is there a lot of confusion over what our job actually entails on the ground and its limits; there is also a gap in understanding what we as snow contractors have to do to cover ourselves from liability. That aspect, Josh says, can sometimes be a harder problem to resolve if the property owner or property manager is set on enjoying the liability coverage they receive from the contractor.

Josh acknowledges that there will always be a push and pull between property owners and managers and contractors, due to the owners and managers wanting to stay under budget, which sometimes means declining services, and a contractor wanting to service it to protect their liability risks. When a property manager has the leverage to decline services and still have their defense picked up in a slip-and-fall claim, the relationship between contractor and owner won't be a good one, especially when a claim emerges.

Another large hindrance to fixing this divide between contractors, insurers, and property owners and managers is the issue of credibility. "Property owners and managers, and frankly insurance carriers too, don't know how to identify a good contractor from a bad contractor," Josh explains. "And because of that, owners and managers put both the public and their own companies at risk. If all they're looking at is who is going to give them the cheapest price for the year, that's not really the best way to do business."

HOPEFUL TRENDS IN SNOWFIGHTING

To recap, bad contractors, unfair contracts, poor documentation by many contractors, and a litigiously inclined public have contributed to a loss of insurers and the subsequent rise in insurance costs, but it's not hopeless. In fact, there's a lot being done and that can still be done to remedy these problems, even more so now than ever before.

"There's a lot of ways to combat it," Josh confirms. "It starts first and foremost with the industry, specifically the snow and ice management industry, taking responsibility for where things are. Whether it's the outside world, insurance carriers, a property owner, or a property manager, they did not know how to identify a good contractor from a bad contractor. There weren't industry certifications, other than a very basic CSP [Certified Safety Professional] certification. There weren't industry standards, and so contractors weren't presenting themselves to the outside world as a professional industry."

The ability for a contractor to prove that they hold themselves to a certain standard goes a long way with property owners, with insurers, and with judges and juries. Bringing these types of certifications on board also involves educating the property owners and managers on how they benefit from a certified contractor and why it is worth paying a little more. It also requires the industry, and hopefully the property owners and managers, to jump on board with some of the legislative reforms to limit the ability to file these claims. Snow and ice management is in a stage of important growth, going from an industry that didn't have much accountability to one that is now trying to flip the script and educate lawmakers, the public at large, the insurance carriers, and the property owners and managers all at once. The changes have been admittedly slow going, and Josh believes that's because the industry didn't approach the property owners and managers first.

Industry advocacy groups "first went to the insurance carriers and then their state senators to pass the tort reform. But I think a better job has to be done educating the property

A better job has to be done educating the property owners and managers about the importance of hiring a good contractor.

owners and managers about the importance of hiring a good contractor. That price can dictate everything, because it's going to protect everybody as a team. [If] you can present great documentation right from the beginning and have a group approach instead of pointing fingers, plaintiffs' attorneys are going to start shying away from questionable cases."

If tackling the problems with lawsuits begins with property owners, then we as contractors need to figure out how to bridge the gap in communication and understanding that too often exists between us. Fortunately, Josh has a few ideas on how to do that.

"The first thing is really making people aware that fair contract language actually benefits the property owner down the road. Fair contract language means giving the contractor some control over the triggers, not just the service trigger but how quickly the contractor has to respond to the site. And fairness in terms of the defense and indemnity provisions—that's a contractor only having to pick up defense and indemnity for a property owner or property manager when they did something wrong."

Josh says that if the contractor and property manager can agree on fair contract language and service triggers, and the manager understands a good contractor from a bad contractor, these claims aren't going to arise as often. One reason for that is because a contractor adhering to the current standards and procedures list is going to pretreat the property, meaning they will push snow in the right directions to avoid dangerous thaw-refreeze issues. They will also conduct preseason site inspections to identify defective site conditions.

Josh also warns of the dangers of trying to defend yourself too late, arguing that both property owners and contractors need to be more proactive about investigating and defending claims from the outset. That means you can't wait until a lawsuit reaches your door to begin protecting yourself, as you're already behind the eight ball as soon as the claim is filed. That is when plaintiff's counsel has the most leverage, because the insurance carrier has to bring in someone like Josh to defend the case. The real leverage on the defense side begins right when an accident occurs. You need to share that information with your team. If you are the property manager on site, and you find out about someone falling, you need to notify your contractor that day and vice versa.

Whether you are the contractor or the property owner or manager, you want your on-site personnel to be checking text messages, photographs, video recordings, phone conversations, and everything you can possibly find to see if they have any information they can share in the defense of the case. Only a small percentage of the time does a defense team have a video of a slip and fall, even when there is a camera on site. That, Josh says, is usually from the lack of an early and aggressive investigation of a claim right upon notice.

If you're a property owner or manager, it's wise to educate your on-site people (i.e., maintenance workers, tradespeople, security personnel, and regular staff) on the importance of slip-and-fall pre-vention *and* lawsuit protection in the snow and ice management world, to ensure they don't overlook something that could prevent an accident or that could be valuable defense evidence. The same thing goes for contractors. You want to educate your laborers about what to look out for, so they can bring it to management's attention if they see or hear something. They won't see what they don't know to look for.

There is one rather simple solution that property owners and contractors could start doing right now, one that Josh believes could be a great defense asset in court: signs. We see Slippery When Wet signs in stores and walkways all the time, and we even see road signs warning of potentially icy road and bridge conditions, but what about in the private snow and ice management world?

"We don't see it very often in defense of the snow and ice management claims, whether it's the contractor or the property owner or property manager," Josh says. "But I think I would like to proceed in a case in which there was signage up that was placed out there either permanently by the owner of the property or put up seasonally for winter conditions or when the snow and ice management contractor is out there. It could be over a large swath of the property or just on the sidewalks, when they do a preseason site inspection, or during the course of the season when they see particular troublesome areas such as sloped areas or depressions. Whatever it is, to put signage up to identify that slippery conditions may exist and to be careful … could absolutely go a long way in defense of a claim. I would certainly prefer that than nothing at all."

Thorough documentation is another critical element to a successful defense in court, so much so that it may determine whether an insurer and a contractor agree to settle or take the case to a courtroom. Documentation is key to a good defense, and so is having certification. Proving that you, as a contractor, have worked to learn and execute a high standard of service, or that a property owner has hired a contractor proven to provide a high level of service, can help sway a judge and jury in times of need.

"If I have an ISO-certified contractor who has all the documentation under the sun, I will fight tooth and nail for that insurance company to let me try the case." When I ask Josh why, he tells me, "Because I feel really good about what a jury is going to think about this contractor who's going out there to keep our roads and our parking lots open for the doctors and nurses and whoever else needs to go out, and this contractor [can] show everything they did, and they're doing it … in compliance with industry standards. I would take that to trial and feel really confident about our chances of winning."

Lack of adequate documentation has plagued our industry in the years since litigious action began to rise, leaving contractors open to all sorts of repercussions simply because they could not prove what they had done and what they had not done. There are, however, a few emerging solutions to this problem, and like most other industries, technology is chief among them.

TECHNOLOGY AS YOUR ALLY

Before he designed one of the best apps specific to snow and ice management, Kevin Speilman was a senior manager at one of Canada's largest mobile carriers in Alberta. There, he was working with oil and gas companies to develop wireless systems that monitor everything from their trucks and crews to wellheads, compressor stations, rig platforms, and more. When Kevin moved back to his hometown of Vancouver to be closer to family, he ended up sharing an office with his brother-in-law, who at the time was running a construction business full time and a small snow and ice management business in the winter. Kevin observed their world in the wintertime—the disorganization, the confusion, the frustration. Struggling to watch something that was fairly chaotic, Kevin proposed they do something about it. That proposal led to Kevin's involvement on the company's systems and technology side and eventually on the business development end of things. What resulted from Kevin's involvement is Yeti, a cloud-based software system that affords users a wide variety of features, including route planning, crew tracking, equipment inventory, record keeping, and more.

Mike Lindenbaum is the founder and CEO of SiteFotos, a field tracking app that allows crews to document their work with time- and location-stamped photos, while also offering site mapping, time tracking, document organization, and more. Invictus started using Mike's product a few years ago, and so far, we've been pleased with how easy it is to keep accurate records of our work, day in and day out.

What makes apps like Yeti and SiteFotos so unique is that they are two of only a handful of software systems available that are specifically designed for snow and ice contractors. "Snow and ice management is our number-one priority, and we don't want to attempt to offer a Swiss Army knife that is going to be diluted for snow and ice. You can use it for other types of business, but our focus internally, and our initial product offerings, are centered on snow and ice," says Kevin.

Companies like Kevin's and Mike's are an important development in our industry, as technology has come somewhat slowly to the world of snow and ice management. Before this type of software, we typically documented our work and directed our crews using paper forms, digital cameras, handwritten notes, or just word of mouth, and certainly many contractors still do things that way.

At Invictus, we still do our job the same way, of course. We do our preseason planning, walk our clients through the contracts, and figure out our resources and who's going to do what by breaking up the work into bite-size pieces. We decide whether to do specific sites internally with our own crews or hire out a subcontractor. Once the season begins and everything is in motion, we have to communicate with those teams, telling them where to go, what to do, and when (often during a weather event), while making sure the sites are serviced properly and all documentation is accounted for. Snow and ice management is a lot more like emergency response than it is like being a plumber or a landscaper. Your best plans usually fall apart on first contact because a snow or ice storm doesn't always unfold how you hope or anticipate that it will. Of course, you plan and prepare for as many different scenarios as you can, but quite often, something unpredictable happens, and things goes sideways.

Kevin saw this firsthand during his time observing his brother-in-law's business. "They had a plan that was documented," he recalls. "They had routes and ways for how they were going to do the work. They had time sheets that guys could fill out. They had little maps so that everybody could see what they were supposed to do. And I would say 20 percent of the time, that worked out. Twenty percent of the time, they had the right map for the right location. They had the right equipment to do the job. They could fill out the time sheet, and then they could get it back to them in a reasonable amount of time so that they could bill the client. And sometimes it didn't have coffee spilled on it or wasn't torn in half so they could actually read what was on the piece of paper and transcribe it into a bill. The other 80 percent is what absorbed an inordinate amount of time and effort to try to sort through what exactly happened."

I'm sure most of the contractors reading this can relate to that scenario a little too well. When the whole flow of data working out perfectly is that rare, something needs to change.

"I would see the fallout the next morning or for the next two or three days after an event, with these guys sitting at a boardroom table sorting through buckets and baskets of paper. Sometimes it was not paper. The ultimate was to watch a two-by-four come in that had notes written on it. It was all the guy could find, a piece of wood in his truck to write down what he did that day. I thought to myself,

'Holy cow.'"

When your documentation is that disorganized, it's really tough to defend your bills to the customer. Let's imagine that a customer tells you they don't believe a worker was on their site for six hours. How can you expect to prove that they were by showing them a time sheet written on a two-by-four? Most contractors, like Kevin's brother-in-law, are very honest, hardworking people who would be happy being left alone to plow snow. It's all the peripheral business administration work that most of them don't think about, either because they're unaware of it or they just don't want to do it. They don't want to think about filling out forms or entering information into an app. They just want to do their work on the ground to the best of their ability. That, as many of them see it, is their job. But it's defending that job and actually tracking their work properly that's always been a challenge for them. Without really good documentation of your work, it can very easily be your word against someone else's. That's not a good place to be for the contractor when challenged by a customer or when up against a lawsuit. That's where simple technology can really help.

A professional organization wants data. They want it because they know that they're doing good work, and the data simply supports that fact. But you should also want data because you want your operation to be better, more efficient, and more secure. How do you really know what's happening in the field, what you're going to change, and how you're going to perform your services differently without good data? Without it, you're just taking a stab at making adjustments because you have nothing to measure against.

Ample data also makes customers happier because there's less questioning of the bill. It makes insurance carriers happy because they know a company has good records to support their case should a claim roll in. But data also helps the organization as a whole do a much better job.

"I think the attitude is shifting," says Kevin. "Good, professional operators understand that they need those systems in place because they are being demanded to do more with less. They have tighter margins or they have thinner access to labor, so they have to do more with less. That's an obvious area that technology can be leveraged for, and it needs to be, if you're going to be successful in this industry, especially in this day and age."

The good news is that tech options are growing in the industry. Companies like Kevin's and Mike's offer a product that is easy to use, and many of them will even provide training services to help get everyone up to speed on how to use the system.

Kevin finds himself in a unique opportunity, given the industry's comparative lack of tech experience as a whole. These days, he's as much of a software developer as he is an educator. "I have a responsibility. If I've created a product that I think is the best for them, then I want to do everything I can to make sure that they see the value (of it) and that they end up using it," Kevin explains. "I don't want guys to stumble along and hit a roadblock because it's too much work or they don't understand and can't get over that bump so they just stop and fall back to whatever thing they were doing before."

Yeti "really is tailored to each company and to what they need. In a perfect world, everybody would sign up, we'd give them the template, they would fill out all their stuff, we would import it, they'd click a few buttons, and then everything would work like magic. That would be wonderful. The reality is most [companies] need two, three, four training sessions with their staff. We need some sessions with their crews, helping them get their guys running on the app. They often need multiple training sessions to get [the system] going.

That's the reality of it."

Another reality is the industry's dire need for this type of help. Historically, the snow and ice industry is not composed of a cutting-edge group of people when it comes to technology. Any technology that does exist has traditionally focused on machinery. Contractors wanted, and understandably still want, stronger plows, upgrades on liquid applications, bigger salters, and better trucks, which is all technology but just not the kind of technology we are talking about here. Today contractors need to be leveraging wireless networks, data and various sources of data, GPS, cloud technology, and other tenets of the digital age if they want to really grow their business. A bigger plow, a better truck, a better salter, a new gizmo—these things are fine, as they help us do the work faster and more effectively. But none of that matters if we can't satisfy our customers, purchase insurance, or successfully defend ourselves from lawsuits. For a company to build and scale in today's environment, adopting a software system and digital technologies for the purposes of documentation, crew tracking, and record keeping is vital.

Now that the technology is beginning to roll in, contractors are wise to jump aboard as early as possible. Even though software specific to snow and ice is relatively new, customers are going to expect you to be using it. They may even expect you to have been using it before you actually were. We have had clients want to withhold payment on past-due invoices because we don't have the same photographic records for our past work as we do for our more current work.

"The challenge is that as soon as one property manager hears about [this technology], their expectations are going to be, 'Well, everyone should be using this,'" says Mike. "And, quite frankly, they're right, but the thought of training a bunch of subcontractor field workers is sometimes a little more challenging. In the real world, people forget to charge their phone, and they show up with a dead phone battery, or they leave their phone at home, or they forgot to pay their bill so they're not getting service that day. Or maybe a guy drops his phone in the snow and it breaks. Until Google's satellites have live video tracking of everything going on, which is a scary proposition, the best you can do is ground the technologies that are out there, within reason, with the good price points, and do your best to train your guys."

CHAPTER FIVE

FRYING PANS AND BLACK BELTS: A LONG JOURNEY TO THE ICE INDUSTRY

Do not call any work menial until you have watched a proud person do it.

—ROBERT BRAULT

Not many snow and ice contractors dreamed of working this job in our youth. You're not likely to hear kids say they want to be a snow and ice removal specialist when they grow up. That's the case, I'm sure, with the vast majority of jobs out there. There can be only so many firefighters, police officers, nurses and doctors, professional athletes, and astronauts, after all.

Having gotten to know many of my colleagues over the last twenty-five-plus years in the business, I know that most of us found our way into the industry by way of someplace else. My story isn't entirely unique in that respect, but I think it is best to give you some perspective on how someone actually becomes a snowfighter. Hopefully my story is a good representation of that journey.

The youngest of three, I was born in Montreal, Quebec, to a middle-class family. My father and mother had what I would call transferable skill sets—as an engraver and a jeweler assistant, respectively—and because they loved travel and adventure, it's little surprise to me now that we moved a dozen or so times before I finished high school.

The first move came before my first birthday, taking us to Canada's western corridor. We rotated through towns and homes around Vancouver for the next several years, and by the time I was a senior in high school, I had been to thirteen different schools. The frequency of change and the familiarity with uncertainty prepared me for life as an entrepreneur, in some ways. I was always curious about what was next, where I could be, and what it might hold in store for me. More importantly, I learned to get comfortable with being uncomfortable.

My parents weren't thrilled by moving, at least not in the way it may seem. They, like most parents, wanted to make life for their children a little better all the time. They didn't change careers, and sometimes they even kept the same jobs. They just wanted a change of scenery, always searching for a home, a school, a neighborhood, a commute, a paycheck, or even a view that was a little better than the one before.

For my part, admittedly, I wasn't the best student. If I had to guess, probably 90 percent of the school changes occurred because of our moving around, while the other 10 percent came from my misbehaving. Ninth grade was particularly concerning because I had to repeat the grade, and I only passed after they added both of my grades together to move me along to the tenth grade. I'm still not sure if my teachers did that out of pity for me or for themselves, but regardless of their motivations, I turned things around when I got to the tenth grade.

I took an interest in cooking soon thereafter, and by the time I graduated two years later, I had a scholarship in the culinary arts. I moved north to the city of Whistler and found work in the restaurant industry as a line cook. But after a few years of working in a hot, windowless kitchen all day and night for next to no pay, I realized that I didn't really want to be a chef after all.

At the time, I was twenty years old living in a large house with about thirty other people. One of my housemates, a guy named Rick Weir, ran a cleaning company, and one night after work, I vented some of my work frustrations to him. "Well, why don't you come work with me?" Rick asked. "I'll pay you twice as much, and you'll work less. You can ski all day and work at night." It didn't take any more convincing than that, since all I wanted to do in those days was ski anyway. I quit my job in the restaurant and started working with Rick cleaning hotels, restaurants, and offices around town. I was making way more money, and I was skiing every day. What could be better?

This was the 1980s, and in those days, in our market, Rick told me that owners were making a hundred grand a year in the cleaning business. I couldn't believe it, and at the end of the season, I decided I wanted to use some of the money I had saved to travel. I ended up traveling for six months, mostly around Australia. While I was there, I realized that

> **I realized that most of the people who were traveling and enjoying life were, for the most part, self-employed.**

most of the people who were traveling and enjoying life were, for the most part, self-employed. That really stuck in my mind as I made my way back home, and it wasn't long before I convinced myself that I, too, would be a business owner by the end of the year.

When I returned to Vancouver six months later, I set out to find what my business was going to be. My first idea was to buy a pressure washer and start looking for dirty houses or buildings. That was my first company, which I named "Pure Pressure Pressure Washing." It was a flop. I didn't get any jobs, and I didn't make any money. It was, to put it mildly, a disaster for my young and somewhat naive ego.

Disheartened, a few buddies and I decided to go camping one weekend in May to blow off some steam. I had a dirt bike strapped down in the back of my truck, and as soon as we drove out to a dirt road, I grabbed the bike and started bombing down the road. I wasn't wearing a helmet, because helmets back then were optional. Within minutes, I wiped out. I landed on my head, and luckily a mud puddle—that was all mud and no rocks—broke my fall. I compressed my spine by 25 percent—a compression fracture, they called it. I was nearly unconscious and in a tremendous amount of pain, so my friends rushed me to the hospital.

It would be some time before I could walk normally again, and to help my progress along, my doctor suggested that I get into some type of stretching and physical fitness regime. I was always fit due to the nature of my work and staying active in my off time, but I hadn't played any sports since high school. Trying out for the local hockey team or even trying my hand at pickup league soccer wasn't exactly at the top of my mind, but exercising in a gym or joining a yoga class didn't fit my style either. Then, the day after I got out of the hospital, I found a flyer on my front doorstep advertising a free introductory karate class. It seemed like a sign. I went, and I loved it. I joined the club that same day and began working out every day afterward.

With my back strengthening daily, I got a job selling Rainbow vacuums. I was a good salesman, often selling one or two vacuums a week and profiting about five hundred bucks per sale. I would make my house calls in the evenings, hopefully make a sale, and then go train with my club. Within two years I got my black belt. Three years after that, I got my second-degree black belt. Then I decided to start my own school with a guy I had met through martial arts, John Fung. We were making money and having fun doing it, but it wasn't good for my family. I had a wife and two small children at home, and my being away every night working and teaching was beginning to wear on my responsibilities at home. The karate run, while fun and educational in many ways, needed to meet its end.

I knew I was good with people, so I decided to stick with sales but branch out of the vacuum business. Coincidentally, I landed a job selling cleaning contracts for two large cleaning companies. It was my job to go out and knock on doors, which I got pretty good at. I was selling enough cleaning contracts to get headhunted by a larger firm, which presented me with an offer that I couldn't pass up. Within a year, however, I realized that while the money I was making from sales was good, it was still just a job. I needed my own company. That was where the freedom was, and besides, that was the dream I had envisioned for myself all those years ago in Australia. Being self-employed was my ticket to traveling for long stretches and working with the people of my choosing. It was time to actually get back on my feet and make the necessary moves toward my original goal before the accident.

INVICTUS IS BORN

It was the summer of 1998 when I registered the name "Invictus" for a business. I was still working my sales gig, and I hadn't really intended on starting my own business, at least not right then. I thought I would work for a year or two more before I actually put the name into action. That plan changed, though, when my boss at the time declined to start service on a job I had sold. When he did, a switch flipped, and Invictus started. Within six months I had quit my job, assembled a small team to clean and service properties, and begun selling on behalf of my own company. We were profitable from day one at Invictus. It just started snowballing, and I remember it as one of the most exhilarating and liberating times of my professional life.

It's funny, those customers that I had way back then—I still have a lot of them today. We've morphed as an organization, of course, but I credit the ability to keep so many of our original clientele to the fact that our approach to business, and to our customers, has remained the same. The aim has always been to be the best, to never be outworked, and to provide the highest quality service or product available. That hasn't changed. We've followed those values, and they've led us to where we are today, through multiple industries.

We began as Invictus Building Maintenance, and then we started adding more services. What started as an interior cleaning business grew into a property maintenance business focused on pressure washing, gutter cleaning, and power sweeping. Then one night in 2004, I had that fateful conversation with my cousin about the snow removal business. After that we were the "master maintenance plan" for customers.

Then, just a few years ago, I pored over our numbers and realized that our snow and ice service was more profitable than any of our other services. Immediately, I knew that we had to change our approach. We had to focus harder on snow and ice management.

We started scaling our snow and ice service from that day forward. We have been working on that for a couple of years, but it wasn't until June 2017 that we decided to drop everything else and devote ourselves completely to snow and ice. Once we made that decision, we officially renamed ourselves Invictus Professional Snowfighters Ltd. Alongside the name change were major changes to our operations. We began shutting down in the summertime, and as hard as it was to do,

> A few years ago, I pored over our numbers and realized that our snow and ice service was more profitable than any of our other services.

we laid off all office staff except for one person. We kept a mechanic and a salesperson on payroll through the summer months and retained a larger seasonal roster from October to about April. The goal today is as clear as it was then: get out in front of our market and industry by becoming a leader in practices, techniques and services, and operational strategies. That's a goal that will keep us pushing forward for the lifetime of the company, a challenge that we are happy to accept, as it keeps us motivated and interested in the work that we do year round.

As the industry adapts to changes in climate and weather patterns, we are faced with both opportunities and challenges. Customers in our market and others must confront uncertain predictions for snowfall and ice, while snowfighters must wrestle with the risks of taking on most, if not all, of the legal accountability for sites they ultimately can't control. But maybe my experiences along the way have prepared me for what lies ahead.

To be a successful entrepreneur, I've learned, is to be comfortable with risk. Some people are afraid of change or hesitate to chase after something whose attainment may seem unrealistic. But, for me, I love that fear of the unknown. I see great possibilities, not impending disasters. I attribute that attitude in large part to my childhood. The frequency with which my family and I moved—having to adapt and readapt to new environments, routines, and people each time— helped prepare me for life as an entrepreneur. I need that uncertainty. I crave not knowing what comes next. It's what fuels me and keeps me fully engaged in my work now. Whatever it is you're fearing, you must tell yourself that it's going to work out until you believe that it will, until you instinctively answer to your own doubts, "Why wouldn't it?"

CHAPTER SIX

TRIAL BY ICE: SNOWFIGHTING IN COURT

Ethics is knowing the difference between what you
have a right to do and what is right to do.

—POTTER STEWART

In the early 2000s, a woman in Virginia was walking from her car
into a convenience store to purchase a newspaper.[4] Rain had fallen
recently, and a small hole in the store's canopy that extended from its
gas pumps to the front door had allowed a puddle of water to settle
on a portion of the sidewalk surrounding the building. The woman
stepped into the puddle, slipped, and fell onto the concrete driveway
roughly eight inches below the sidewalk's surface. A witness later
claimed to have seen the woman's head snap backward as though she
had been punched directly in the face by a boxer. The woman went

---

4   Alan Cooper, "Woman wins $12.2M verdict for slip-and-fall outside store,"
     Virginia Lawyers Weekly, May 7, 2007.

to the emergency room and received stitches for a gash on her chin. She did not report losing consciousness or any other side effects, and as a result, the hospital did not check for any brain damage.

Over the next few months, however, the woman began experiencing short-term memory loss, fatigue, dizziness, balance issues, stress, and depression—symptoms of a mild traumatic brain injury. She struggled to run her business and ultimately lost it and became emotionally withdrawn from friends and family. The woman sought legal counsel, and together they decided to sue the convenience store for negligence. A number of medical professionals, friends, and family members testified on the plaintiff's behalf, and several of the store's employees admitted that they had known about the leak for quite some time and had failed to warn customers about the dangers of stepping into the puddle. After hearing the case, the jury retreated into a private room to deliberate their verdict. While they mulled over the case, the plaintiff's attorneys and the defense team negotiated a settlement in which the plaintiff would receive no less than $1.5 million in damages but no more than the defendant's insurance limit of $6 million. But when the jury reemerged, they delivered a verdict that stunned both parties involved: a whopping $12.2 million in damages for the plaintiff.

If you ask ASCA executive director Kevin Gilbride about the biggest problem facing the snowfighting industry, he doesn't need to think about it for long. "It's frivolous lawsuits," Kevin says. "It is unfair claims. It's unfair transfer of liability." While the case above did not involve a snow and ice contractor, it is an example of the type of unpredictability involved in slip-and-fall cases as well as the enormous cost they can incur on whoever is held liable—hence, the rising insurance costs. In recent years, a number of snow and ice companies have exited the industry simply because they cannot obtain insurance.

Kevin isn't the only one who sees the effect litigation is having on the industry. Most industry experts agree that the biggest problems contractors face in the snow and ice business today stem from lawsuits. Due to the litigation risks, insurance costs are rising drastically, a reality that is forcing a great number of reputable snow and ice professionals out of the business. To make matters worse, the number of unethical and desperate contractors is rising, as many try to do the job without sufficient insurance or, as is in some cases, without any insurance at all.

Once a party files any type of slip-and-fall claim, it's illegal for the snow contractor to withhold it from their insurance provider. Whether it's legitimate or not, the claim will be recorded in their insurance history. As a result, the contractor may face immediately higher premiums and deductibles, and they will be penalized when they renew their policy. The ASCA estimates that 76 percent of contractors pay a deductible per incident, with 28 percent having a deductible between $1,000 and $2,000. Nearly half of all contractors report deductibles less than $1,000, meaning that roughly 23 percent of contractors pay deductibles in excess of $2,000 per incident.

After an insurance carrier receives documentation of a claim, contractors reported that 34.5 percent of claims filed against them were dismissed. Despite their dismissal, however, the claims often still bring about rate increases when it comes time to renew the policy. Other times, even a dismissed claim can result in the cancellation of the contractor's policy by the insurance provider. New carriers may insure them, but it's common for the contractor to see their rates rise from 50 percent to 300 percent. Deductible rates also rise, with some charging as much as $10,000 per incident.

The ASCA estimates that a little more than half of all undismissed claims are settled out of court, 72 percent of those for less than $20,000. Such cases are referred to as *nuisance payments*, and they are made according to the insurance company's assessment of a claim's potential costs (i.e., legal expenses and plaintiff costs if they lose the case).

The remaining 15 percent of slip-and-fall claims go to trial, affecting contractors in several ways. "First, they pay their deductible, a real cost," Kevin explains in his report. "Secondly, the insurance company sets aside a reserve amount of money they think they could pay out in the event of the lawsuit being found in favor of the plaintiff. That amount is often $250,000. When their insurance policy comes up for renewal, that $250,000 is counted as an actual loss for the policy, and the insurance rates are increased accordingly. Lastly, the time spent out of their businesses costs them money."

The ASCA found that more than half of snow contractors pay up to 3 percent of their total snow revenues to insurance costs. About 62 percent of contractors received rate increases due to slip-and-fall claims. And perhaps most shocking was the discovery that 56.6 percent of snow contractors reported that those rate increases were between 10 percent and 30 percent in one year alone.

"The standard insurance carriers have all but stopped insuring the professional snow and ice management industry, and excess insurance carriers are now walking away as well," Kevin explains in his report.

From this perspective, the disastrous recipe becomes clearer. The combination of frivolous or bogus lawsuits, increased insurance costs, and a growing shortage of insurance providers has put the entire professional industry under threat of extinction.

THE BURDEN OF LIABILITY

Kevin and the ASCA have worked since 2012 advocating on behalf of snow and ice contractors for more favorable legislation and support in an industry that is often undervalued and overworked. For as long as the industry has existed, it seems, snow and ice contractors have been shouldering the legal risk of keeping safe a site that they rarely have any control of.

"It is the snow contractor's job to protect themselves, their companies, their clients, and their insurance carrier," Kevin explains. "In order to do that, you have to follow certain processes and procedures that will enable you to defend a claim two, three, four, five years down the line."

Those procedures require a snow contractor to re-create exactly what happened on every property, at every time they were there, in the event of a lawsuit. Let's suppose that your company receives a claim for an incident on January 12 at 2:32 in the morning. You need to be able to tell the attorneys who, if anyone, was on the site; prove that you trained those people on the site adequately; and answer for what they did when they were on the site, what time they got there and what time they left, and what sort of equipment was operating on the site.

"You look at this industry, and it's a very fragmented industry," Kevin says. "All you need is a pickup truck and a plow, and suddenly you're in the snowplowing business. But are you really a professional? It's one of the challenges with this industry. You also have all kinds of customers and buyers out there, and what they try to do is save money. They're trying to get the best service, presumably, for the least amount of money at the same time. They're probably also trying to do it with the least liability, which is where you get into some real tricky areas."

Those tricky areas revolve around the business of a property owner passing on the liability of the snow and ice management company through a contract and then not allowing them to plow. A property owner can legally say that the snowfighter is responsible for any and all incidents, accidents, and injuries on the property, yet they can tell the snowfighter that they can't come out until there is three inches of snow on the ground or that they are not allowed to put salt down. If you sign a contract with such terms, and there's an inch of snow on the ground, you are liable, even though you're not getting paid and you can't go out and plow snow.

The ASCA is combating high insurance premiums—as well as the reluctancy to insure snow companies at all—by working to institute quality control standards across the industry. Since Invictus earned its ISO 9001/SN 9001, we joined a small group of companies to be counted as verified professionals, a first for our industry. By ensuring the highest quality of work, the ASCA hopes that the cost of insurance premiums will stay down, because the insurance carrier will be able to defend the accredited company more easily in the event of a slip-and-fall claim.

So far, the strategy appears to be working. Of the 30,000-plus annual claims for snow-related slip-and-fall lawsuits in the United States and Canada, 35 percent of them are dismissed outright, usually because the contractor was able to prove that they did what they were supposed to do and get them and the property owner out of the case. A small number of the claims fall to the property owner's responsibility (in states with laws that hold property owners account-able), usually due to negligence. The rest, according to the ASCA, are either lost in the courtroom or they settle outside of court. "They're nuisance suits, intending for a quick pay-up," says Kevin.

For ASCA-accredited companies with their ISO certification,

however, roughly 70 percent of all claims against them are dismissed. ASCA works only with companies that follow their policy of documenting every site extremely thoroughly while also adhering to the highest quality operation standards available, with the intention being not only a better service but also a better legal defense should one be necessary. The insurance company that ASCA works with, Mills Insurance Group, can make money again, and ASCA members end up saving money after their premiums go down because they're a safer bet to insure.

These standards are the result of a collaboration between ASCA and the American National Standards Institute (ANSI). In January 2014, the ASCA released the first set of industry standards for snow and ice management. These standards were accredited by ANSI and recognized by both the US and the Canadian court systems as a legitimate and recognizable accredited standard.

The documentation that ASCA requires from its members is detailed in the standards, and then to back it up, companies that are ISO 9001/SN 9001 certified have an independent third party that comes in annually to audit their processes and procedures to ensure service quality and that they have implemented and are abiding by the industry standards.

A more uniform and credible industry was all part of the plan from the beginning for ASCA. "We started in 2012," says Kevin. "Our mission then and now was to influence the outside world, to make the snow and ice contractors a more professional industry. In doing so, we based it on the four pillars of ASCA."

Those pillars begin with written industry standards. Having a set of quality control dictates is what enables the filtration process for new members and regulates their membership from induction. This is one of the most important features of an ASCA membership. By knowing and proving that your company adheres to these standards in its operations, the ASCA and the associated insurance agency can better protect you and your company against lawsuits.

The second pillar is education, which is mostly focused on an individual-based certification for snowfighters. The third pillar is verification, which is the ASCA's ISO 9001/SN 9001 certification. This is, in a sense, the ASCA's quality management system. Finally, the fourth pillar is legislative change. The ASCA works diligently to enact legislation at the state level and at the provincial level in Canada to tame the bullying, so to speak, from property owners and local governments as well as defend against fraudulent and frivolous lawsuits.

MEETING ACCREDITED STANDARDS

Once a company is certified by the ASCA as an accredited snow and ice management entity, it has to prove that it meets certain quality standards required by the ASCA's accreditation rules and that the company did what it was contracted to do should a conflict arise. We do this at Invictus by using a number of different technologies to monitor every crew and site we are responsible for around the clock and to document all activity on every contracted site. We do that to maintain our accreditation and to protect ourselves against a bad claim. If a property owner assumes that we are taking on all the liability, then they can tell us when to plow or salt and remain free of liability in the event of an accident. Obviously, that puts us in a position where we have to determine how much risk we want to take on or if we even want to take on the risk at all.

In doing so, we are making a decision that potentially renders lawsuits that aren't our fault, which can potentially cost us our insurance and even our company. Every snow and ice management company has to make this decision for themselves, but few actually know exactly what they're taking on and how much they are risking. Inescapable debt, bankruptcy, and even jail time are all possibilities, depending on the circumstances and one's legal outcomes.

Many companies, especially smaller ones that are just starting out, will sign a terrible contract out of sheer excitement or desperation. Maybe a company got a large account, such as a chain of supermarkets or the state park, only to discover later that it's being sued because someone injured themselves in a slip and fall. Whether it was the company's fault or not, now it must defend itself in a lengthy and costly court

> **Many companies, especially smaller ones that are just starting out, will sign a terrible contract out of sheer excitement or desperation.**

battle. For snow contractors, we can continue playing this game until every insurance company leaves the marketplace, or we can try to change the laws. The latter option is now the main role and mission of the ASCA.

"We just had the law passed in Colorado," says Kevin, his tone proud and energetic. "We sat down with the building owners and explained to them the situation. Our deal was, 'Listen, we don't want to get rid of the snow contractor's liability. That's not what we are trying to do. We just don't want to take on *your* liability.' They said, 'What do you mean, our liability?'

"'You can't tell us not to plow and hold us liable.' Every single one of them looked at us and said, 'That doesn't happen.' I pulled out three contracts and said, 'Yes, it does.'"

Every property owner present at that meeting read the contracts

Kevin had placed on the table and concluded that the current practices were unfair and needed to change. It's what Kevin calls *logical legislation*.

"It just takes time to get these things going," Kevin explains. "We are fighting back because we want an amicable relationship between the snow contractor and the property owner. We want you [the contractor] to be able to sit down and say, 'OK, listen, you've got a budgetary issue. You want to spend $400,000 this year on snow. I get it. There are ways we can get you to that. We buy the insurance policy, but we can work on it as a partner, and that way when you drive in here in the winter, you know you've paid me and I'm going to protect your butt if we both get sued.'"

In other words, when the property owners know the insurance conundrum the snow contractor is in, they can (and usually do) see the benefit in helping the snow contractor do their job free of inter-ference. "The property owners need to understand that they're not hiring a snow contractor; they're hiring a risk management partner," says Kevin.

> **The property owners need to understand that they're not hiring a snow contractor; they're hiring a risk management partner.**

We are one of few industries whose workers and work remain relatively invisible to the consumer. You may see us during a daytime storm, but for the most part, we work when most people are asleep, and our work is usually noticed only when it's not done rather than when it is. It's a somewhat unappreciated and mysterious line of work in that way, which makes it all the more important that the consumer is well educated on what we do as well as what threatens us. After all, it will soon threaten them too if we can no longer do our work in a responsible way.

CHAPTER SEVEN

THE INSURANCE DILEMMA

The secret of change is to focus all of your energy, not on fighting the old, but on building the new.

—SOCRATES

For the snow and ice industry, companies generally run into one of two problems with regard to insurance, if not both. They either can't get insurance because they don't have the processes and procedures in place to best manage their book of business, or they can secure insurance, but they can't keep up with the costs over time. There are a few roots to the legal and insurance problems for the snow and ice industry. For starters, there is no Standard Industrial Classification (SIC) code for snow and ice management. An SIC code is what the government and private firms use to classify an industry. Because snow and ice management is a seasonal business, companies were lumped into a property management classification regardless of whether they were solely a snow and ice company. When insurance carriers entered the picture, they were generally selling a landscape policy, a power sweeping policy, or an excavating policy that also covered snow. That changed in 2011 when, for the first time ever, insurance companies started looking into their policy arrangements because they could not figure out why their landscape and janitorial policies were starting to have their margins squeezed so tightly. You can imagine the gasp that might have erupted when they realized how much they were losing from snow and ice related lawsuits.

The shock reverberated through the insurance industry, and eventually contracts with near-impossible restrictions began to pop up with greater regularity. These types of contracts define a long list of exceptions to coverage, which are generally referred to as *ineligible risks*. Says one such contract that an ASCA member in Pennsylvania received, "Snowplow operations being performed for the following types of risks are ineligible: hospitals and medical centers; rehab facilities; nursing homes; assisted living facilities; retirement communities; public transportation and housing including airports, bus terminals, and rail stations; schools, colleges and universities; retail box stores; and shopping malls." What's left, your front yard? Well, in a way, yes. The contract goes on to stipulate that "snow operations being performed for the following types of risks are ineligible if the client does not have the landscape lawn care contract for the same property. That is, condo and homeowner's association, the apartment complexes, strip malls greater than one hundred parking places, banks, credit unions, and hotels and motels."

In other words, they will insure your company only if you also do landscaping on the property for which you are seeking coverage.

Insurance companies know that landscaping policies are generally profitable, so they're hoping to hedge their bets against the riskier snow coverage. The problem is that the difference between landscaping and snow removal is black and white. It's oranges and apples. They're two totally different trades. It's like hiring a team of carpenters to put out a fire. A company leaning more toward landscaping is far less likely to have the best methods and techniques in snow and ice management, yet it is far more likely to acquire insurance coverage.

The ASCA is currently working at the legislative level to gain better options for snow and ice companies and their insurers, but their efforts are not without opposition. The ASCA's model legislation that's currently being passed around congressional hearings in several states essentially prevents a property owner from keeping an indemnification clause or a hold harmless agreement for the sake of passing their liability onto the snow and ice management company.

> A company leaning more toward landscaping is far less likely to have the best methods and techniques in snow and ice management, yet it is far more likely to acquire insurance coverage.

In 2015, the bill passed the House and the Senate in Illinois with unanimous support. On August 25, 2016, Senate Bill 2138 was signed into law by Illinois governor Bruce Rauner.

The victory encouraged the ASCA to take the bill to other states, and for the last few years, they have introduced it in Colorado, Michigan, New Jersey, New York, Ohio, Pennsylvania, and Indiana. In the last session, it got as far as passing the House in Michigan and all the way to the Senate Committee hearing, but it failed to pass before the bill's sponsor's term ended.

The bill passed in Colorado, but it failed in New Jersey. On the plus side, it's moving through the ranks well in all other states where it's been proposed, and it's been resubmitted in Michigan and New Jersey after further negotiations with the sponsors' respective opponents.

With the legislative protections that stem from the bill, snow and ice contractors will have better terms in their contracts, leading to less liability and greater insurability. The ASCA, for its part, is looking to build a better infrastructure around its legislative wing, beginning with a better funding mechanism and more effective ways to present its legislation.

These changes to the law aren't unfair to the property owner either. "We are very, very careful to explain both sides very thoroughly," says Kevin. "The one side, which business owners and the conservative legislators seem to lean to, is the business argument that it's unfair. They see it as, 'If you were using my insurance policy, essentially, for your gain, and my insurance was going through the roof, that's not good business, and we need to fix that.'"

The other side of the argument surrounds public safety. A lack of liability and the power to deny a contractor permission to service a site creates a serious safety issue. Without the incentive to maintain their properties properly, you would be surprised how many property owners won't. From a government's perspective, a problem that is bad for business and a threat to public safety is a problem that takes priority. Because of that fact, the concerns that so many of us in the snow and ice industry have had for years are finally getting heard.

INSIDE THE INSURANCE DILEMMA

Noah Sherman is a regional vice president at Mills Insurance Group, often cited as the number-one snow and ice insurance agency. He has spent the majority of his career working with snow and ice companies to find solutions for their insurance problems, and he's one of only a relative handful in the North American insurance trade who still is. Very few know more about the snow and ice industry's insurance dilemma than Noah, and even he stresses how complicated and case by case the problem really is.

"Unfortunately, there's no easy answer," Noah says of the industry's shrinking insurance options, "because a lot of the carriers that are writing [coverage] are looking for different things. The insurance world is, unfortunately, a little bit slow moving to catch up with the times and with what we are trying to accomplish. So different ones are on different legs of that race. Obviously, from any insurance standpoint, it's always going to be about control, safety, and stability. There are various degrees of how far into the operations different carriers are going to look. The ones that are looking a little bit further into the operations are the ones that are getting the most success. Unfortunately, there are still some carriers who just aren't taking an accurate snapshot … which is leading to a lot of problems."

Noah says that carriers who failed to understand the industry and their needs are primarily the ones exiting from it now. Some were more invested in other industries or types of coverage from the beginning and simply did not have a strong grasp on the complexities pertaining to snow and ice coverage. Others might have had a firm understanding of the industry at one point but ultimately grew distant from it and thus were less aware of the changes in litigious activity and other factors that have caused a need for coverage standards to evolve.

Today, you see carriers that will pop into and out of the snow and ice industry because they didn't anticipate the challenges that are somewhat unique to our field compared to other trade industries. Carriers that dip their toes into the water and then jump back out often leave snow and ice companies vulnerable and scrambling to find another carrier. Then you have the carriers who have been in the snow and ice game for a long time but who are so committed to doing things a certain way that they refuse to change their ways and end up having to get out of the industry due to mounting costs. Regardless of their reasons for why they exit, they weren't accurately assessing the risks. That lack of knowledge led to carriers either opening themselves up to exposures they were unfamiliar with or undercharging for the exposures they were picking up.

Of course, contractors are always looking at their premiums. As business owners, we know the importance of both insurance coverage and our bottom line, which is why we tend to look for the lowest premium possible. It just seems like a solution to both of our concerns—two birds, right? But sometimes the lowest premium is actually a bane to the contractor or to the carrier. If just one slip-and-fall claim can take out years and years of premium earned and the policy is no longer profitable for the carrier, then they are likely to drop the coverage and get out before they take a loss. That's a common problem in our industry, and Noah says it occurs so frequently because so many carriers lack the understanding to charge adequately, and so many contractors want the cheapest policy.

A WORKING SOLUTION FOR INSURERS

What about the insurance carriers that stay in the snow and ice industry, the ones like Mills that seem to be withstanding the increasing risks of insuring snow and ice contractors with comparative ease? What do they know that these other carriers do not? What's their formula, and why is it working? I went to Noah to find out.

"Mills, as an agency, has been able to stay in it just because of our expertise and the way we approach it with an understanding [of the industry]," Noah explains. "We keep our finger on the pulse through our involvement specifically with the ASCA and with snow contractors across the nation."

When other insurance carriers began running out of the industry, Mills decided to go in even further. It was a bold move, one that was so full of risk that many of Mills's competitors thought they were dooming themselves. But Mills saw an opportunity where few others did in the emergence of the ASCA, an organization that was dedicated to progressing the snow and ice management industry through education, standardization, legal representation, and solidarity. They got in on the bottom floor, so to speak, and played an integral role in writing the standards that the ASCA uses today.

Mills understood that if they could standardize the industry, they could better protect both it and themselves. In fact, when Kevin Gilbride first called on some of the biggest snow and ice contractors in North America all those years ago to discuss challenges facing the industry, he began by asking them what they felt were the three biggest problems in their business. The unanimous answer, as Kevin recalls, was "insurance. Insurance. And insurance." Noah remembers those days as well.

"That was kind of Kevin's wake-up call," says Noah, "where he realized how big of an impact [insurance] was having. He actually reached out to us, and we partnered with the ASCA, so we were involved in creating those standards and still work with the ASCA very closely to maintain them, update them, and do our best to help in that fight and effort."

Those early meetings marked the first time that major players in the snow and ice industry and members of a prominent snow and ice insurance carrier actually came together to discuss how they could work jointly to combat the growing threats of litigation and the rising costs that are associated with it. If Mills was going to stay involved in the industry, they had to make sure contractors knew how to protect themselves as liabilities began to stack against them. It was a case of "help me help you" and vice versa, which led to the standards that ASCA-certified contractors follow today.

MINIMIZING RISK THROUGH DOCUMENTATION

When I ask Noah what the most critical risk-mitigating piece is for contractors, he, like Josh Ferguson, doesn't hesitate. "Documentation. That's a huge buzzword around the snow removal industry, especially around the ASCA. Documentation is really just always going to be the name of the game. When push comes to shove, the outcome that we are looking for is a closed-out claim. All of this is going to be revolving around any kind of claim—property damage, slip-and-fall claims, or anything like that—because that's what is going to be paid out or not paid out."

> When I ask Noah what the most critical risk-mitigating piece is for contractors, he, like Josh Ferguson, doesn't hesitate. "Documentation."

I think I speak for most contractors when I say that one thing we are always trying to improve on when it comes to documentation is the amount of data we collect on a site and the quality of that data. The quality of data that we are collecting from crews in the field can vary widely. How we capture it and how we store it efficiently have also long been problems. That's why it's important for contractors to know what types of documentation insurance carriers and lawyers want from them.

"There can never be too much documentation," Noah says. "A lot of contractors nowadays are using technology. Baseline [documentation] is a tough thing to gauge, but obviously any kind of logs for time in and time out, accumulation, weather conditions, work performed, etc. is good. But really it's going to be a matter of any kind of physical documentation that can prove when you were there and the work that you performed. Any kind of pictures, GPS tracking, a lot of my clients are starting to use dashcams in any of the trucks or mobile equipment that they're using. I've had a number of clients that have been outright saved from having to pay out a claim because of a dashcam proving that a lawsuit was completely frivolous."

Noah also advises contractors and property owners to be conscious of the laws surrounding statute of limitations in their area. In most places, a plaintiff has three to four years to bring forth a lawsuit, and most plaintiffs' attorneys will use that to their advantage. For instance, if the statute of limitations is three years, they will wait two years and three hundred sixty-four days before they file their claim. They're hoping that by letting as much time lapse as possible before they file, the contractor or property owner will lose some documentation or just not remember it accurately. All your documentation (i.e., videos, photographs, documents, recorded phone calls) should be kept on file for at least the length of your area's statute of limitations.

INSURANCE AND THE PERFECT STORM: A FOUR-PRONGED PROBLEM

From the perspective of most within the insurance industry, the insurance dilemma came in the form of a four-sided assault. On one front, litigious pressure was mounting as a result of bad contractors doing poor-quality work and opening themselves and others up to rightful personal injury claims as well as good contractors failing to document their work. Unscrupulous lawyers and members of the public quickly followed with frivolous or false claims. In response, unfair contracts that pinned most or all liability to the contractor came at the behest of skittish or domineering property owners and managers. And finally, minimally engaged insurance carriers who were unprepared for the wave of risk collapsed, leading to high coverage costs and few carrier options.

"When I describe the history of how we got to this point, I always talk about it in three or four different fingers to point, if you will," Noah explains. "Certainly the litigious nature of our society right now is a huge contributing factor. We do presentations in which we have a picture of an LED sign up outside of an attorney's office that says, 'Slip and Fall Claims $20,000.' You know they are advertising as if it is almost free money. Unfortunately, it's become way too commonplace."

Noah reiterates that the lack of documentation, the total or partial absence of any way for the contractor to prove that an accident wasn't due to their negligence, contributed heavily to the recent rise in claims. Seeing that most contractors were insured and that they weren't great at keeping the sort of records that could defend against a personal injury claim, some lawyers saw the industry as a sitting duck, so to speak, too easy to win settlements against for them not to go after contractors for a quick twenty grand.

Once the lawsuits came rolling in, the financial risks exacerbated debates between property owners and contractors over who was liable for what on their site and when.

"Property owners had been passing down far too much negligence, or in some cases all of the negligence, to the contractors," says Noah. "They were forcing them to sign these contracts that basically said, 'Everything is your fault, no matter what.' That's beyond unfair. That's another front that we are always going to be trying to attack, is trying to get a little bit fairer contracts being signed. That's the big bill that the ASCA is trying to pass, to eliminate hold harmless agreements that unfairly pass the negligence down to contractors."

That doesn't excuse contractors from signing bad contracts, of course, but we know that people can shop around until they find someone who is desperate or unaware enough to sign a bad contract. Noah also understands that some risks need to be taken as a contractor, especially when a company is just starting out and wants to build a strong reputation.

"I always tell my clients that I'm never going to try to stop them from growing their business. I can't tell you not to take on properties, because it's how you make a living, and it's your money. But it can cost you a lot too. At what expense are you willing to risk it?"

Insurance providers began creating a formula for what to charge a snow contractor, which usually consisted of plugging in a set of general figures (e.g., income, payroll, and size of fleet) to determine individual deductibles and premiums. That method didn't come close to accounting for the many differences that exist from one market to the next, much less from one business to the other.

"Insurance companies are the fourth finger to point," says Noah. "They just weren't rating these things accurately, and many refused to catch up with the times. Then there was the classic tale of insurance companies paying out claims because it's cheaper to pay them than it is to fight them. That takes us back to the encouragement of slip-and-fall claims. The plaintiff's attorney can find that threshold where it's cheaper to pay it out than it is to fight it, and then that's how much they'll sue for. Far too often, it works too well."

A JOINT WAY OUT

Despite how we got here, though, the reality is that we are here, and whether you're a contractor, property owner, or an insurer, it's a very bad place to find yourself. It's not so bad for these types of plaintiffs' attorneys and their clients, of course—so long as they don't run everyone out of the business. Whether you're a contractor, property owner or manager, or an insurance carrier, it doesn't benefit anyone to point fingers solely to place blame. But just like anything else, it's important to look back at the history to find the missteps that got us where we are. We can right the wrongs and make sure we don't make the same mistakes moving forward, but we first have to acknowledge the mistakes.

Fortunately, Noah and his team at Mills see a united front coming. It's a matter of getting everyone on the same page, which is far easier said than done, but it is beginning to happen. That is one of the primary goals of organizations like the ASCA. They are trying to standardize the industry to get everyone on the same page in terms of what quality, defensible work looks like. Doing that, however, requires contractors to voluntarily pursue certification and maintain its standards. It also requires contractors to push back on unfair contracts. If both the property owners and the contractors agree on a specific set of standards for the work, then negotiating negligence liability will be far less complicated and hostile. It's an alliance that's already taken hold in Illinois, where in 2018, one major property management company became the first in North America to require ISO-certified companies for all of its snow and ice management contracts.

Not all property owners and managers care about certifications, of course. Some care only about the cheapest, least liable contract they can get signed. In Invictus's early days, we encountered property owners or property managers who would give us the ultimatum of signing their contract or telling us they would find someone who would. Fortunately, we are at place now that we can turn down bad contracts and say, "If it's our negligence, we'll take it on. If it's your negligence, you take it on." The main reason we can do that is because of our reputation for high standards that we built as a company over many years, which was bolstered significantly by our certifications and our full-year, sole focus on all things snow and ice management.

It's not just contractors who benefit from industry standards and fairer contracts, though. It helps ensure that the property owners and managers receive the best service possible, too, from properly insured companies with well-trained crews. That's a change that Noah is already starting to see take place as well, with more national property management companies coming to the table to negotiate more sensible contracts for their properties.

In fact, several national property management companies are even helping the ASCA to pass bills in the state senates in every state to abolish hold harmless agreements that would hold the contractors responsible for everyone's negligence, regardless of the contract's stipulations.

The classic example of how this type of contract hurts the contractor is the two-inch trigger clause, in which the contractor is required to come out and plow only when there's two inches or more of snowfall on the ground. Let's say there's a slip and fall at one inch, and the injured party files a claim. Even though the contractor was never supposed to be there to begin with, as per their contract, the hold harmless agreement finds them negligent anyway.

Invictus stopped accepting contracts that dictated when we could service the site a few years ago. If we give clients a presentation on the seriousness of this situation right now, more often than not, they're willing to negotiate contractual terms that share some of the liability or at least let us service the site when we know we need to. They understand that if the insurance companies can't continue to cover us, then they're going to lose all quality snow and ice contractors, and there won't be anyone to do a job they depend on greatly.

The bottom line is that the risks associated with this job are great. I think all the players involved are beginning to realize that fact. More property owners and managers understand that they're not just hiring a guy to cut lawns anymore. This is a real need for public safety as well as an industry that's become extremely vulnerable to frivolous slip-and-fall claims. Those two realities are sinking in and changing how we see each other, and in effect, how we do business together.

For property owners and contractors alike, when you start hearing that an industry is proposing certification requirements, more training, and a deeper education in subjects like commercial insurance and law, you start thinking about costs. Noah has heard these concerns before, and he doesn't sugarcoat his predictions for the short-term effects of these changes.

"I think it might get a little bit worse before it gets better," Noah says. "But if we can see the industry normalize itself, we can see the insurance premiums start to decrease—because a lot of the contract prices going up are because the contractors are having to account for their insurance prices. But also, part of the professionalism may be that they're requiring more man power, more training, more salt, more trucks, or something else. They're going to incur a lot of costs along the way to becoming more professional … it's going to be a slow process. It's like an ocean liner making a turn. It's going to be many small turns along the way, but we are starting to see them happen."

Of course, the cost to the end user for a contractor to perform a higher quality job is to be expected. The New York Fire Department probably has a *little* higher overhead than the Syracuse volunteer department. At the end of the day, if you're a contractor running a business that you can't make any money from, then what's the point? The same can be said for the insurers.

"It kind of parallels with the professionalism of the contractors," explains Noah. "As far as carriers go, only the strong are going to survive as well. It's not something that you can just try your hand at, and I think it's going to be a long time before we see anybody else come in with any longevity. I think in the past two years, we've seen about six or seven different carriers who were some bigger-name players get out altogether. Before that we saw them tightening their guidelines or trying to scramble to change the way they were doing things to salvage their programs, but it just didn't work. We are seeing more of them drop out, and nobody's filling that void. Next year we may see an influx of carriers who are coming in and want to try their hand at this. But, again, only the strong are going to survive. As long as the insurance carriers are slow to catch up on how they're rating and how they're taking a look at the exposures, I think it's going to be a while before we see any serious longevity."

There is no single person or group to blame for this dilemma, one that is spreading into three industries at once. But it's important for contractors to keep in mind that some of the insurance problems they're facing are caused by the things some of us still don't want to face. Lower premiums, better coverage, and fairer contracts require a collective effort to drive more professionalism into our work and a more unified approach in how we run our industry.

As contractors, we have a number of answers to rectify the insurance problem. We have our standards now. We have our ISO certifications and our technology requirements. We have organizations like the ASCA working to change state hold harmless laws. But what about the property owners and managers who are looking for proper coverage but maybe can't or aren't willing to pay for it? What should they do?

"The lowest bidder is not always the best," Noah says. "And so there needs to be some willingness to have some flexibility there as well as doing a thorough job of vetting who you're working with. As the industry starts to become more professional, there are designations that snow contractors are able to get now. And that goes a long way. It separates people. The ISO certification is obviously a very high accolade. It differentiates contractors. [Property owners and managers] should be vigilant and not just focused on price—and be willing to participate along with the contractors to try to normalize the industry."

CHAPTER EIGHT

SALT: WHY IT'S SUCH A PRECIOUS COMMODITY OF THE TRADE

The cure for anything is salt water—sweat, tears, or the sea.

—SWEDISH PROVERB

There are few, if any, materials more important to snowfighting than salt. It's the main deicing agent for our industry, and without it, roads, sidewalks, parking lots, and bridges would be impassable during freezing temperatures and wet weather. Each year, road crews spread approximately sixty-six million tons of salt on roadways around the world. US road maintenance departments alone pour roughly nineteen million tons of salt on its roads.[5] In Canada, the

---

5   Greg Breining, "We're Pouring Millions of Tons of Salt on Roads Each Winter. Here's Why That's a Problem," November 6, 2017, https://ensia.com/features/road-salt/.

group Environment Canada estimates that between one and a half and four million tons of salt were spread on roads throughout the country between 2004 and 2015, taking into account the severity of the winter.[6]

The use of salt in the snow and ice industry has a fairly long history, dating back to the 1940s as automobile accessibility grew and road travel became more popular. But why, after nearly seven decades, is it still the primary weapon against icy roadways? That's a question that deserves a deeper look.

THE HISTORY OF ROAD SALT

Salt has been important to civilization since the beginning of time. Empires have been built and lost on salt's behalf. In fact, some historians believe that many of the first large civilizations in human history developed near deserts because salt was easier to find and harvest there compared to wetter regions. It's even played a central role in stoking warfare, once famously pitting the Duchy of Ferrara against the Republic of Venice in a bloody bid for the region's salt trade. The word *salt* itself hails from the spice's worth. The Latins reportedly paid individuals in salt, also known as their *salary*.

Salt is also vital to human life. We need salt for digestion, blood, sweat, tears, nerve transmission, and many other functions.

Today, salt is used for everything from seasoning food to preservation to cleaning to medical treatment. Second only to chemical production, though, no industry uses more salt than the snow and ice management business. In the United States, salt was first used to deice roads in New Hampshire, after the state began experimenting

---

6   Andrew Russell, "Why do we still use road salt and what are the alternatives?" *Global News*, January 11, 2017, https://globalnews.ca/news/3174300/why-do-we-still-use-road-salt-and-what-are-the-alternatives/.

with granular sodium chloride to prevent icy roads in 1938. Four years later, in the winter of 1942, transportation departments spread roughly five thousand tons of salt on highways across the country. That number rose consistently each year as more and more cars hit the road.

Before the use of salt as a deicer, governments typically spread sand and cinders (smoldering wood, coal, or other material) around roadways in an effort to increase tire traction. Drivers were also expected to affix snow chains to their tires, or in many cases, simply stay off the road when it was snowing or icy outside. After the Second World War, however, North America's highway system exploded. Industrialization was in full effect, allowing for vehicles that were both more efficient and capable of long-distance travel as well as more affordable. The boom in vehicles on the road gave way to a fast-expanding highway system. Delivery trucks, commuters, vacationers—people took to the road in droves. Within just a few years, travel had become a crucial component of the national economy, and right alongside the rise of travelers was the rise of road salt use.

The bare-pavement concept, in which motorists expect roads to be free of all snow and ice shortly after a weather event, became standard in most cities and their surrounding areas throughout North America by the 1950s. Along with that expectation, it's estimated that salt use doubled every five years throughout the 1960s and 1970s, with salt usage ballooning from one million tons

The bare-pavement concept, in which motorists expect roads to be free of all snow and ice shortly after a weather event, became standard in most cities and their surrounding areas throughout North America by the 1950s.

in 1955 to nearly ten million tons less than fifteen years later.[7] A major factor for that increase was the fact that salt began to replace abrasives like sand, as government agencies and private snowfighters increasingly adopted salt for the chemical benefits that kept roads free of ice rather than minimally improving traction atop the ice.

By the 1970s the transition from abrasives to salt was nearly complete, and right around that time, people began to notice salt's adverse effects on vehicles, roads and bridges, wildlife, and the environment. As a result, automobile manufacturers and structural engineers began researching rust-resistant materials, and governments began rethinking their salting practices. Whereas salt had once been chucked from the back of large trucks by men with shovels, innovations in equipment and techniques brought us mechanical salt spreaders. Beginning in the 1950s and 1960s, discs and rollers that stretched the length of a truck's bed allowed operators to more evenly, and easily, spread salt over a wide path. It wasn't long before snowfighters realized that if they laid windrows of salt—much like you see a farmer creating rows of crops—they could use less salt and still break the pavement-to-ice bond. Soon after that innovation, salt brines came into wide use, in which the snowfighter dampens the salt with water and sprays it onto the roadway. Brines are easier to distribute, since the salt is not as affected by wind or passing traffic as dry salt, and they also break up the ice faster because the salt dissolves more quickly.

Governments and snow and ice companies have worked together to perfect spreading equipment and establish official salting policies over the last four-plus decades. As a result, annual salt use has stopped the dramatic rise seen in the 1950s and 1960s, and according to the

---

7   Transportation Research Board, *Highway Deicing: Comparing Salt and Calcium Magnesium Acetate* (Washington, DC, 1991).

National Research Council, has since oscillated from roughly eight million to nineteen million tons over the last few decades, depending on winter conditions.[8]

SALT AS A DEICER: WHAT IS IT EXACTLY?

What we call *salt* in snow and ice management refers to road salt, also known as *rock salt*. It's mostly sodium chloride, chemically abbreviated as *NaCl* (*Na* is the chemical abbreviation for sodium, and *Cl* is the abbreviation for chloride). Road or rock salt is the same stuff you use in and on your food. The only difference between table salt and road salt is that the latter form has been kept in larger chunks, hence the alternate name *rock salt*. Road/rock salt and table salt are still composed of the same molecular properties—sodium chloride—but table salt is finely ground and purified, and additives such as iodine and anticlumping agents are usually added to the mix to ensure that it's safe for human consumption and to make it easier to use in the kitchen. Road salt, on the other hand, is kept raw, and its grains are much coarser than your standard table salt or even a mixture such as sea salt.

Contrary to popular belief, road salt does not actually melt ice upon impact. Instead, when it dissolves into water or slush, salt actually lowers water's freezing point, preventing ice from forming or reforming. Because salt prevents water's molecules from joining together to create ice, the water maintains a slightly warmer temperature than the ice and eventually melts it. So, salt is effective at melting ice, yes, but it doesn't happen immediately. What made road salt king among deicers in our industry is twofold: price and efficiency. Salt is, for the most part, the most affordable option in large quantities,

---

8   Ibid.

and the fact that it's fairly easy and fast to put down makes it the best deicer in the eyes of most snowfighters.

SALT PRODUCTION: WHERE IT COMES FROM

With all the millions of tons of salt that we require each year, where does it come from, and how do we get it into our trucks and spreaders?

According to Virginia-based trade association the Salt Institute, there are three main ways to make salt. Manufacturers produce solar salt by evaporating seawater, a process that typically involves the sun and large earthen ponds called *condensers*. The energy to evaporate the water and raise the salt concentration to the point of crystallization, which the Salt Institute measures as 25.8 percent NaCl (or on the Baumé scale, which measures the density of a range of liquids, 25.4 Bé°), comes directly from the sun and wind.

The water slowly becomes more saline until it resembles a kind of brine. Then it is moved through a series of ponds for as long as two years. Once the brine has reached the desired crystallizing level, it is poured into crystallizing ponds, where it continues to concentrate. Once crystallization is complete, the pond is drained of the extremely concentrated magnesium brine (referred to as *bitterns* due to its taste), which is either discarded or processed for other minerals. Finally, harvester equipment scrapes up the layer of salt crystals, moving them to an area where they are washed in clean brine, crushed, and sometimes dried in kilns or specially designed driers.

Table salt, or evaporated salt, is the highest purity grade of salt. It is harvested through a procedure known as *solution mining*, in which water is forced underground to dissolve the salt beneath the surface. Once dissolution is complete, the brine is recovered and sent to a plant similar to what you would see in food processing. The solution is then placed in "pans" or tanks, where it is essentially boiled until it is crystallized into salt.

The third type of salt is rock salt. This is the stuff we prefer to use in the snow and ice industry. It is mined "dry," meaning workers actually use blasting and drilling to extract crystal salt from large underground deposits in the earth, which formed from the evaporation of ancient seas. Miners descend underground through shafts approximately twenty feet in diameter, tunnels that can reach depths as great as two thousand feet (609 meters) below the surface. To put that into perspective, that's close to two hundred stories below ground. Once they reach the deposit seam, workers break apart slabs of rock salt with dynamite and powered shoveling equipment. Trucks then carry the salt to a system of conveyors and crushers where the salt slabs are pulverized into small bits. A large, well-functioning mine of this kind is capable of extracting up to nine hundred tons of salt per hour.

Mines such as these exist all over the world, but it's actually the United States and China that produce the largest amount of the world's salt. Together, the two countries supply 40 percent of the 250 million tons of salt that is produced worldwide each year.

NEGOTIATING THE SUPPLY: SALT DISTRIBUTION AND HOW IT'S USED

Most snow and ice professionals start their season with well over the amount of salt they think they'll need. You never can be too prepared when it comes to salt. Without it, our job is incredibly difficult and costly. Most snowfighters will tell you that they keep their salt stock somewhere between 125 and 150 percent. We store the salt in large warehouses or outside under blankets of tarps to keep the supply dry. If our supply runs out, as happened to me in 2016, we do anything and everything to get more.

In Invictus's case, Vancouver was hit by an unexpected and particularly nasty winter storm one season that took the whole region
by surprise. Snow and ice companies, city officials, salt suppliers—
everyone was in a panic to get more salt. Many of our clients didn't
understand why their properties weren't getting the kind of service
they were accustomed to because they didn't understand the critical
relationship we snowfighters have with salt. With most of the city
without any salt stores left, we resorted to paying a hefty price to
buy salt from several hundred miles away and having it shipped in
by train. We bought twelve train cars' worth of salt that year to deal
with the high demand.

Marc Gibson is the national sales and marketing manager for
Mainroad Group, a leading provider of products and services in
the civil infrastructure sector across Canada. Marc and Mainroad
are our main salt supplier at Invictus, so I sat down with him and
fellow snowfighter Dale Martin to learn more about how salt sales
are negotiated, how salt is transported, and where they typically get
their supply from.

Back in 2016, Mainroad saved the day for many local government departments and businesses. The supply shortage was the result
of terrible weather and the poor planning of one of the major salt
suppliers in our region. When that company's supply ran out, the
British Columbia authorities put pressure on Mainroad to supply
noncustomers, mainly regional municipalities. For the sake of public
safety, Mainroad had to cut off some of its own customers for a short
time to comply with the demands and ensure the safety of road travel.

As far as the global supply is concerned, Marc is not too worried
about it for good reason. "It's pretty hard to run out of salt globally,"
he says, "because a good chunk of the volume of salt that's purchased

throughout the world comes from the ocean. There are salt mines inland in most continents, but the majority of pure deicing salt comes from the ocean."

Marc is right. Scientists estimate that salt comprises 3.5 percent of the weight of the world's oceans.[9] "We're not going to be running out of salt anytime soon. Let's put it that way," Marc says with a laugh.

Once sea salt, or solar salt, is ready, it's placed on ships and moved to wherever it's needed throughout the world. "It's pretty much as pure as you get coming out of the ocean," says Marc. "On the other hand, you've got potash salt (a mined or manufactured salt containing potassium), which is basically a by-product of potash mining that you'll find in Saskatchewan and throughout central parts of the United States. You've also got a salt mine in Goderich, Ontario, which is the biggest in Canada."

The mine in Goderich, it should be known, is the largest underground salt mine in the world. It was discovered in 1866 by crews searching for oil. Today the mine rests approximately 1,750 feet (533 meters) below the earth's surface and spans 2.7 square miles (7 square kilometers), even reaching under Lake Huron.

"Those are your two basic ways of getting salt," explains Marc, "either a natural sea salt or mining it inland. Volcanic ash salt is going to be a different color and have different properties."

As it pertains to snow and ice management, Dale is an expert, having started in the industry in 1975 and dedicated his adult life to learning everything he can about the tools and techniques of the trade. If you ask Dale, there are different ways each type of salt should be used as a deicer.

---

9   "Why is the ocean salty?" National Ocean Service, accessed August 13, 2019, https://oceanservice.noaa.gov/facts/whysalty.html.

"Potash is like a pink powder, and it's obtained through the mining. It's a by-product, a waste product that they actually recycle. The difference between that and straight salt is the elapsed times. So, for example, with potash I would hold off putting it down in anything that has temperatures dropping below -15°C. That's where I would have to either put it with the winter bracer and blend it in when we got into colder temperatures, because ice would just refreeze. With straight salt, or rock salt, you can go up to about -21°C. But your elapse time on rock salt takes a lot longer. It's not salt that melts the road; it's the brine. You could throw salt all over the road, but if it doesn't get any moisture, it will go off in the shoulder, which then affects your vegetation." Not to mention not melting the ice.

"Fraction salt, what we call the old-fashioned rock salt, was the best alternative when it came to between that and potash," says Dale.

When it comes to salt shortages, Dale agrees with Marc that there should be no concerns of ever running out on a global scale. We all see news story after news story during the winter months of salt shortages, complete with mobs of people rushing to a dump truck with buckets and shovels to grapple with one another for a few scoops of the sandy salt mixture public works departments so often use. Or we read about how the city's salt stores are nearly depleted after a heavy storm, and no matter how irrational we may know that it is, for a split second we find ourselves wondering if we'll ever be able to drive the roads again this winter. Dale sees through the hysteria and remains calm about the situation.

"I think a good chunk of that is the unpredictability of what your season's going to be like weather wise and how much salt you're going to go through. From what we've seen in the last few years isn't so much a shortage from the mining standpoint; it's more of a shortage from who has the most inventory and who forecasted properly. And forecasting salt is pretty difficult on an annual basis. I couldn't tell you what the weather is going to be like two weeks from now, let alone three months from now when I need to have it in stock, right? So basically, you're running your inventory off of historical averages, and then from there, if you run into a season like in the lower mainland in 2016, no one's prepared for a year like that. In the lower mainland (Vancouver's region), you deal with a month of weather total throughout the winter that you're going to really need to worry about salt. Spread that out over three or four different events. In 2016, it was two months straight. And so when you're talking about a shortage of inventory at that point, it takes time to resupply."

Most of the salt that suppliers in Invictus's region get comes from Central and South America, such as Mexico and Chile, or from North African countries, such as Egypt. It doesn't come overnight. It takes quite some time to mine it, process it, package it, and then ship it here. Once the ships arrive off the coast, they set anchor and off-load the salt onto trucks and trains, which carry the salt to area stockyards. There, the goods are tarped and stored safely away from the elements. When a municipality or snow and ice business like Invictus places an order, the salt is loaded onto large trucks and delivered directly to the customer. So, by the time you're starting to run short, it can take some time to get more. If everyone else is running low too, then you could enter into an outage period, similar to what happened to Invictus and most of the other companies in the lower mainland in 2016.

How long on average does it take to get salt from one of the big mines? Unfortunately, that's a question with too many variables to answer the same way every time it's asked.

"If we really, desperately need it and the ships are in the right location at the right time, it can turn around two weeks to a month," Marc says. "That's if everything works perfectly. Really, for us, we're planning about three months out to have everything ready to go and get that process started to get all the salt shipped up here."

Because Marc and his partners at Mainroad Group deal directly with both independent snow and ice management businesses and large city and state public works departments, they see the causes of a salt shortage as multifaceted, although it's usually owing to poor planning.

"Cities are ordering large quantities of salt," Marc explains. "When there's a crisis, it's usually that a city runs out because they didn't order enough or because they got a worse winter than they expected, and then their supplies run out. To be fair, they sometimes use a little too much when they didn't need to, but on a global level, we're not going to run out of salt. It's not going to happen ... There's a chance that the future is going to have another year where someone overpromises on volume and runs out in a harsh winter again. Did we learn something from that year [2016]? Absolutely. I think everyone in the lower mainland learned a lot from that year."

When I asked fellow snowfighter Jason Case about any issues he's noticed with regard to procuring salt, he explained just how inter-connected the trading of salt is with the rest of the world's natural resources markets.

"We struggled with shipping and receiving," says Jason. "Suppliers not being able to get enough shipped to bring the salt [to Boston] from overseas, whether South America or Morocco. Back when China was absorbing a lot of the ships to haul steel, there wasn't a lot of haul back for products like salt. That was a major challenge, and now a major challenge is, of course, winter itself. Nobody really knows how much supply to bring in to support all of their customers throughout the season, whether it's going to be a light season or a heavy season.

"When it's a heavy season and all the salt yards are absorbed with customers, states and municipalities pretty much come in and take over. The private sector ends up taking a back seat, unless you're a very powerful buyer. That's another challenge. All this is a supply-and-demand issue, which certainly affects price. That is, I would say, the third largest challenge. Supply and demand really dictates the price."

Despite plenty of supply, because of increased demand due to the unpredictability of weather, rising prices become a major concern for everyone. "It falls back into, 'How do you plan ahead for this?'" says Marc. "Dale talks about utilizing the coats on cows and horses [animals getting thick coats early in the season can indicate a colder-than-average winter] as well as the *Farmers' Almanac*. People are looking at the La Niña and El Niño years. You do what you can. You're pretty much looking at every forecast that exists and trying to figure out which one is right, which one is wrong, and how much do we have to really prepare to bring in."

If a contractor or city depletes its salt supply during an unexpectedly bad winter, most likely it will have to buy salt on the open market, where prices can easily double. That financial stress on municipal budgets and small businesses alike means other government needs can't be met, and for some snowfighters, it could mean a loss of business or worse. For that reason and the environmental, mechanical, and public safety concerns regarding the use of salt, there has been more of a focus on alternatives in recent years, whether as a backup option or as a full replacement.

What are the alternatives? The notion that salt's popularity may be waning among the public is lost on no one in the snow and ice industry. Since the 1970s, the negative effects of salt have made headlines and been the subject of debates as far ranging as legislative battles in government to individuals complaining to one another about the rust on their cars. In cold climates, we all feel the impact of salt.

"The thing with salt is, it's perceived as an environmentally damaging product," says Marc. "That's the perception of it. Asphalt and concrete deteriorates due to more salt usage and everything else of that sort. These are all things that the public is seeing. And so, we have to be aware that there's going be environmental impacts from the government aspect. New regulations will come into play on how we dispose of it, how we store it, water runoff, everything of that sort. That's something that we have to deal with on a daily basis on how we control that, and if I'm going to predict anything here, I think that's going to start moving its way down to the final end user as well, at a certain point. I think that's something we should be prepared for, in ensuring that all of our storage locations are really up to speed on how we dispose of it, where we're storing it, that it's tarped, proper drainage, etc. We've noticed this over the last many years, that environmentally we're dealing with a lot more restrictions when it comes to salt usage. We have to be watching for that."

So, what are the alternatives, and do they really work? Finely ground sand is an option, though it does not melt ice and only slightly improves vehicle traction. In desperate times, however, it's much better than nothing, and it's easily accessible and affordable. Beet juice and cheese brine, as well as salt-based brines with low concentrations of pure salt, are other options that we're seeing more often, particularly in Canada. The Salt Institute doesn't have data on how many cities are actually using these alternatives, but there is a growing interest in the products due to their relative effectiveness (compared to sand, cinders, fertilizer, and the like) and the fact that they're largely environmentally safe. These substitutes will not eliminate the need for rock salt, but snowfighters are increasingly adding them to their arsenal in the event of a salt shortage or if they have to service a particularly sensitive area. Dale estimates that his company will use approximately 600,000 liters of brine this year.

"Beet juice was found by an accident," Dale explains. "If you can find a product that's 100 percent organic and reusable, you'll make yourself a billion." With that thought in mind, a farmer, as the story goes, had a realization one day. "He was just spreading (beet juice) in his fields," Dale says, "thinking it would make a good fertilizer. Instead of purchasing fertilizer, he had noticed that his beets did a good job of fertilizing. He [sprayed the beet juice] in wintertime when it was starting to snow and realized that it kept the fields from freezing. That's how it all started."

The alternative caught wider attention when it was learned that beet juice could not only prevent ice from forming but that it was also less corrosive than salt. Sodium chloride (i.e., salt), as it turns out, is not the only molecule that can keep water from crystallizing. The sugar molecules in beet juice have a similar effect, although not quite to the same degree as sodium chloride. Snowfighters soon realized that if beet sugar is added to a 20 percent salt solution and sprayed on ice, the melting point of ice actually lowers to below 15°F. The tackiness of the molasses in beet juice, though inconvenient for shoes and cars, also helps the rock salt stick to the pavement.

There have been some issues, however, including some environmental problems. If beet juice seeps into waterways, the sugar fosters bacteria that sucks up enough oxygen to disrupt the ecosystem and can result in the death of fish and plant life.

Dale also pointed out that one of the biggest issues with beet juice is its color. "One hundred percent beet juice is red, and it was tracking on vehicles and hard to get off the vehicle. When they went straight beet juice in Edmonton, on the ring road [beltway] and the tarmacs they got a lot of complaints about it because it would track so bad." Red roads, snow piles, shoes, and cars do have the appearance of a horror movie (not to mention a sticky cleanup). White beets and the use of calcium in the mixture have since been introduced, but the stickiness and hazards to waterways remain.

Jason has also pondered the use of salt alternatives, such as liquid deicers, but he notes that there are too many problems in the distribution infrastructure to make it a viable replacement of salt.

"People right now can drive over to the local salt distributor and load up with salt in the back of their hopper and then go spread it," explains Jason. "You can't drive to those same locations and get liquid deicing material. The entire supply chain of the product has to invest tens of thousands of dollars in either making it, buying it, stowing it in silos, and being able to off-load it. Then, how do you charge for it? You charge by the gallon like a gas station, with a pump? That infrastructure just doesn't exist for your everyday contractor to go get liquid. I see that being a major obstacle for a lot of snow and ice contractors and probably a main reason why they say, 'Hey, I'd love to use liquid, but I can't go get it. I can't make the investment to buy a full trailer load of it.'"

Until these and other alternatives are perfected and put into wider use, however, they are a costly substitute. Nothing as of yet can match the affordability and the effectiveness of old-fashioned pure rock salt.

Salt saves more lives than any current alternative.

Above all, salt saves more lives than any current alternative. A study by Marquette University in Milwaukee, Wisconsin, revealed that road salt reduced crashes by 88 percent, injuries by 85 percent, and accident costs by 85 percent. A second study conducted by the University of Waterloo in Ontario and released in 2014 found that there was a reduction of 51 percent in collision rates before and after salt application. The study also discovered that the number of collisions decreased by 65 percent when salting was combined with plowing.

Safety is obviously the biggest factor in the use of salt, and given that fact alone, it's very unlikely that snowfighters will stop using it any time soon. But changes in the industry occur every day, and they don't always come from within. Suppliers like Mainroad, snowfighters like Dale and me, and property owners and managers have to keep an eye on the changes swirling around us, such as road-surfacing technology, smart vehicles, the oil industry, government regulations, and more.

"In the kind of business that we're in, I think you have to be involved in understanding what any new technology that comes into play is," says Marc. "It can change your industry overnight."

CHAPTER NINE

THE PROPERTY MANAGER'S PERSPECTIVE

The fact that an opinion has been widely held is no evidence whatsoever that it is not utterly absurd.

—BERTRAND RUSSELL

I am a snowfighter. I run a snow and ice management company. As such, I know that my field of vision is going to stray, to one degree or another, toward the issues affecting snowfighters and snow and ice business owners—those like me. I don't, however, want to leave out the views and needs of the property owner and manager. This is the group I would like to speak to the most after all, since property owners and managers are generally looking for any and all ways to improve the services they need. Similarly, contractors are generally trying to improve their services while also explaining why and how it must or should be done this way or that way. Common ground is needed, and that can come only from a mutual understanding of the walls we're all up against and where they stand between us. So I reached out to Wayne Lee, a successful property manager in Western Canada and a good friend of mine for many years, to get his input on what contractors need to know about the work of a property manager.

Wayne has spent most of his adult life working in real estate and property management. For the last fifteen years, Wayne has served as a respected property manager in the Vancouver area, working with such firms as Bentall Retail Services, Bosa Development, and Colliers International. He is currently the vice president of the Gulf Pacific Group's Property Services division. I've known Wayne personally for roughly two decades, and through our many conversations together, I know he's a property manager who understands the importance of snow and ice management. But, like all property managers, Wayne has to hire, monitor, and ultimately be partially responsible for the work of dozens of contractors. Obviously it's impossible to be an expert on every industry you have to hire from, which is one reason why standardization is so important to property managers. The more they know up front about who the reliable professionals of a particular trade are, the easier their job is.

"In the property management business, we rely heavily on service contractors to provide a service—be it janitorial, be it landscaping, be it snow removal, be it electrical or HVAC maintenance, or something else," says Wayne. "I don't really separate the fact that we don't hold them any differently as a snow removal contractor. They do have their scope of work. They do have their terms and conditions and their specs. But from my perspective, I look at as, 'If you're going to provide a service, what is that service? What are you going to charge for that service? And when are you going to perform that service?' If you can meet all of those requirements and keep all those promises, everything's good."

In other words, a property owner wants to know that a service provider knows three things: what your job is, how much it will cost, and when the job will be done. That's the fundamentals of the business relationship between contractor and property manager, but it's certainly not always as simple as that.

"We look at reputation, pricing, and reliability—can they do what they say they're going to do? Certificates are definitely qualifications. Reputation just comes from referrals, past performance, and relationships with the contractor," Wayne explains. "We get calls every week from different contractors wanting to do business with us, like any property manager does. We probably get a dozen calls a week from different contractors who are not working for us right now but want to. We could spend all day talking to these people, but sometimes our day doesn't allow for that. So we have to know who to hire and who to keep. I look at it as a property manager's success is in the contractors that back them up. 'Back them up' meaning the contractor's performance reflects on the property manager."

> **A property owner wants to know that a service provider knows three things: what your job is, how much it will cost, and when the job will be done.**

Wayne also understands that the contractors he and his team hire and manage are an extension of their own firm, and the work we do as contractors is a reflection of his work as a property manager.

"The eyes of the tenants that are in our buildings, they don't see us out there working. They see our contractors, who we hire. They are a representation of us in the sense that they're here to make the building look good and at the same time make us, as property managers or property owners, look good. Because if the property looks good, people just assume that it's being well taken care of. If it's not, then some people accept that. We don't; we want it to be attended to. We want it to look nice. We take pride in the properties that we manage, and the performance of the service providers bears on that greatly."

Unlike the workers whose job it is to interact with the public, most contractors are rarely actually seen. It's our work that is visible or felt, and that poses some unique challenges for us, in the sense that our work can often be taken for granted until it's not done. When that's the case, rarely does anyone other than the contractor understand why it wasn't done. That can be a difficult expectation to juggle, for both the contractor and the property manager who must answer directly to the property owner, any of the property's tenants, and the public.

"Snow and ice management is a night or early-morning job," explains Wayne. "Nobody actually sees them, but they do see the results. They either see the salt spread on the road or the sidewalks or the snow cleared out of the way and the site being left accessible, or they don't. They don't have to physically see them do it, much like landscaping. Half the time they don't see landscapers, yet the landscaping looks nice.

"You walk into a shopping center; you never see anybody working in there other than the retailers. You don't realize that there's a team of ten people that are actually making sure the lights are on, the floors are clean, and the roof isn't leaking. When you walk in, you get this expectation that it's going to be warm, it's going to be lit, and it's going to be clean. Typically these services are invisible. But if I show up at my office or my shopping center in the morning, and I can drive in and park and walk through the parking lot without slipping or walking in snow, I'm thinking, 'This is wonderful.' I didn't see the guy do it. I don't need to see the guy do it. But this is one of those invisible services that if it wasn't done, you're going to notice."

Unlike most services, snow and ice comes with an uncertain timetable, something property managers often dread. A major part of their job is to keep everything flowing in an orderly fashion, and that's significantly more difficult if one of your most important services doesn't know when they'll need to access the site, for how long, at precisely what cost, or how inconveniencing their work will be at any given time. Because nothing else moves if the property is inaccessible—no deliveries, no customers, no workers, no other service providers—snow and ice removal is critical to a property's functionality. And yet, it's the most unforeseeable service for the property manager.

"Snow and ice is totally unpredictable," Wayne says bluntly, "especially if you compare it to an HVAC contract or a janitorial contract.

Because nothing else moves if the property is inaccessible—no deliveries, no customers, no workers, no other service providers—snow and ice removal is critical to a property's functionality.

A janitor knows he has to go in every night and clean an office. A landscaper knows he has to go out every week and cut the grass and trim the bushes. The HVAC guy knows that every quarter he has to go change filters and tighten belts and check electrical and flow and everything else. But the snow and ice [contractor] is in a unique situation in that sense. Number one, it's for three, four months a year, and Mother Nature is unpredictable.

"The biggest challenge I see for snow and ice companies is around how to gear up for it. You have people on standby wanting and willing and able to work, yet if they don't work, they don't get paid. Whereas the other service contractors have a regular schedule. They know, for twelve months of the year, they're going to be doing this *X* number of times, and they can develop a contract and their compensation to reflect that. Whereas with snow removal, things are unpredictable."

Wayne is right. As a snow and ice contractor, the weather plays the biggest part in our job, unlike most other jobs. We can lose by not having enough snow and ice in a given season just as easily as we can lose by having too much of it. Even though we've worked very hard at creating a seasonal rate that is a win-win as much as it can be, you still have variables to contend with that are completely unpredictable. For instance, it's a semifrequent occurrence to have a crew out servicing on a very mild night, which we classify as a "low-risk night," only to have them encounter a somewhat irregular weather issue given the climate, such as black ice, that we have to send backup out to help deal with. On the flip side, a contractor can sit there for four months and not do anything before, all of a sudden, a snowfall dumps several inches over the city.

Surprise or not, we have to be Johnny-on-the-spot and make our sites perfect within hours. That's where the planning comes in to play. That's why we scrimmage all the time, so we'll be prepared and execute our mission smoothly whenever those random events occur. It's an imperfect scenario, especially in our market, but that's why planning and training year round are so important. That uncertainty is also a thorn in the side of a property manager's ability to budget for their clients, but it's not one that Wayne is too concerned about, given the importance of snow and ice management and the impossibility of predicting its expenses with perfect accuracy.

"Snow removal, in its unpredictability in nature, is an easy variance to explain—although people do forget," says Wayne. "If you have a really bad winter, by the time [the owners] get their bill in late spring, they might have forgotten what the winter was like. But it's one of those variables that is necessary and understandable. I don't care about snow personally, because if it snows, it snows. You have to deal with it. If you blow your budget because of a heavy snowfall, like I said, it can be explained, whereas you start trying to explain another variance in HVAC, it gets a little more complicated. Snow is one of those issues that everybody knows is unpredictable. Everybody knows that when it does fall, havoc breaks loose. Everybody knows that, because they also had a hard time getting to work. [Property owners] know that it's going [to] be an expense that they're going [to] have to absorb and incur. A set monthly rate helps property managers budget. For our area, we use an average based on five or so saltings per month and a couple snow events. Judging by that is our minimum [budget]. If it ends up being less, great, because then we'll have a surplus of money at the end of the year. But if it ends up being over, and we had a really, really harsh winter and we doubled the budget, like I said, as long as we are justified, then it's an easy one to explain."

BUILDING AND STRENGTHENING RELATIONSHIPS

The relationship between snow and ice contractors and property owners and managers, like other industries, can become strained at times. Property managers typically have a full plate overseeing a wide array of responsibilities for each site they manage, from navigating government regulations to hiring contractors to managing on-site staff and more. It's a tough gig as it is, and given the rather nocturnal nature of a snow and ice manager's job, Wayne says a successful partnership depends a lot on how well he and his snow and ice contractors understand one another's jobs.

"Communication is key, I think, especially during a snow event," says Wayne. "Ice is ice. Usually you have to have a little more time to plan for ice. You don't have too much time to plan for snow, and sometimes it snows more than they predict. Other times it doesn't snow at all. So the ups and downs of that, from a contractor's point of view, I think are tough. The commitment is to have a lot cleaned by 10:00. And then by 10:00 it's still pouring snow. So while the lot was cleaned … the perception is that it wasn't done. And then you have the other issue of a contractor saying, 'Well, I did it once at 9:00, I'm doing it again at 12:00, and I'm doing it again at 6:00, so all of a sudden I'm doing it three times in one day versus one.' Everybody knows it's required, but is it easy to swallow? It never is."

Wayne says that ideally, property managers would like to know that the snow removal contractor has a crew waiting to do their site as soon as it stops snowing and as soon as it starts snowing. But in reality you can't have that many people on standby all the time, everywhere.

"If you could do that, there wouldn't even need to be a discussion," says Wayne. "That's exactly what everybody wants, but the reality is … it's unrealistic. That's why communication is so critical."

CHAPTER TEN

BEFORE YOU CALL
A SPECIALIST

It's hardly a secret that a disconnect often occurs between the professional tradesperson and their customer base. It's no different in the snow and ice management sector, with the knowledge gap existing mostly between the snowfighter and the property owner or manager. The average snow and ice contractor doesn't know much about what a property manager does, and the average property manager doesn't know much more about a snow and ice contractor other than that they make their property safe and accessible for traffic. If a property owner or manager can drive to their property in the morning but can't enter the parking lot, then they know their contractor didn't do something right. But for the most part, that's the extent of their knowledge on what separates a good snow and ice contractor from a bad one. Understanding the role of a property manager doesn't fare much better from the contractor's perspective either. In fact, the typical dynamic between the two parties is perhaps best described by a sentiment you're likely to hear from either side, "They think they know it all, and we are pretty sure they don't know anything."

It's a rift in communication that often leads to countless misunderstandings, poor service by bad snow contractors, unfair contracts by uninformed property owners/managers, and ultimately a lot of lost dollars on both ends. It's not uncommon for property owners and managers to think of the snow and ice contractor's job as a commoditized service they can get from anyone with a truck and a plow, unaware that one needs any amount of expertise or training to do the work. We know that this could not be further from the truth, because if someone doesn't know what they are doing, they are going to put snow in the wrong place, use the wrong deicing materials, fail to service the site when needed, and a whole host of other mistakes. In the end, they are going to create more problems than they solve. The uneducated contractor is almost as dangerous as the uneducated property manager, and when they come together, the result can be catastrophic.

THE QUESTIONS YOU SHOULD KNOW TO ASK

Every year, you're likely to hear of a few horror stories from the land of snow and ice management: disgruntled workers quitting in the midst of a storm. Regular people trying their hand at clearing poorly maintained roads or parking lots only to injure themselves, damage property, or find themselves on the wrong side of the law and facing a fine or a lawsuit. There was even the 2017 case of a man in Washington piling loads of snow against the doors and across the entranceways of a gas station because the owner declined to use his snowplowing services. Bad "professionals" in the snow and ice management industry are no rarer than are bad conditions or misinformed members of the public. The good news is that much of this can be improved upon simply by learning a little more about what to look for in an honest, competent, and dependable professional.

From learning more about the various weather conditions (i.e., what they mean to snowfighters and how they affect our work) to learning some of the basics about our industry's history, equipment, and techniques, a solid educational foundation can help save a countless number of hours, dollars, and gray hairs in the long run.

I don't say this from a far-off place of presumption either. For many of my customers, the world of snowfighting and all the work that it entails is something of a mystery. That gap in information often leads to misunderstandings and unrealistic expectations about our services and costs, which ultimately hurts us both. To better educate them, we developed a series of questions for our sales team to ask new clients in an effort to gauge how much, or how little, a potential client may know about the industry.

A few of these questions cover industry-related news that, believe it or not, many people *within* our industry would be surprised to learn. For instance, we'll ask, "Did you know that there's an ANSI-certified standard for the snow and ice management industry? Did you know that fewer and fewer insurance companies are going to be insuring the snow and ice management due to high risk and bad business practices? Did you know that there's something called an ISO 9001 SN available to the snow and ice industry?"

For those types of questions, the majority of respondents tell us that they were unaware of industry certifications, standards, and the growing insurance concerns. It's important to note that the SN 9001 was created by the ASCA as an extension of the ISO's 9001 program. The SN 9001 is a quality management system specifically designed for the snow and ice management industry, but it remains in conjunction with the existing ISO 9001. Contractors earn ISO 9001 SN certification through an independent, third-party audit that examines the contractors' processes and procedures to assess service quality and their adherence to industry standards. Invictus is the first (and currently only) snow and ice management company to obtain its ISO 9001 SN certification in the Pacific Northwest, but more contractors around Canada and the United States are beginning to seek their own certifications in recent years. The reason behind that, I suspect, is that they have seen how helpful it is in easing customer concerns, obtaining and retaining insurance, and streamlining operations and training.

Most customers don't know about these programs, much less the notion of such a thing as snow and ice industry standards. We got so much feedback from customers telling us that they did not know what our certification meant and that they hadn't heard about the insurance-related issues facing the industry, that we made it our mission to educate them. We've taken steps already to meet with our customers through the summer and fall for an educational series designed to teach them what the standards of snow and ice management are and how we plan to meet them for their sites. If they know what the standards are, then they know what to look for, not only in our work but in the work of others as well. If they know that insurance companies are getting tighter and tighter on who they will actually insure for snow and ice and how that will affect them, then they would see the benefit in working with us to try to solve the problem.

We've taken steps already to meet with our customers through the summer and fall for an educational series designed to teach them what the standards of snow and ice management are and how we plan to meet them for their sites.

We are starting to see that, since more and more companies are operating with these standards and doing business properly. As a result, the risks are much lower and thus so are the insurance costs. If customers actually want an insured snow removal company, they have to know that this is where the trend is going. That's where we are right now. We are on the trend of change, and people are hearing about it. We are making sure they hear it as often as possible, that the snow and ice business is doing things differently today than it was five years ago.

People are interested in progress, and when that progress leads to improvements, they tend to get more invested. We want to get the industry and those it serves excited about change, so we are doing everything we can to promote the concept that good standards equal lower costs and safer, better sites for everyone. But it's hard to make an idea stick if you don't know the full story, beginning with where these standards and the idea of snow and ice specialists in the modern age really come from.

TO UNIFY AN INDUSTRY: THE STORY OF STANDARDIZING SNOW AND ICE MANAGEMENT

In 2018, an Illinois-based company became the first large-scale property management company to require its contractors to have ISO certification. Since the beginning of the industry, no other large property owner or property management group had required such a certification for its snow and ice management contracts. For many, myself included, that decision is a bellwether for the change we can expect to see across the industry, a coming evolution in the way contracts are designed and issued that will require some dramatic changes for snowfighters.

No one, in my opinion, knows more about how and why the

snow and ice management industry has evolved over the last several decades than John Allin. John is perhaps the most prominent thought leader in the snow and ice industry. He's been called the "godfather of snow and ice," and I wouldn't disagree with that title. His list of pioneering accomplishments is long enough to fill their own chapter, so I will just give you some of the highlights.

John got his start in the industry by building the largest landscape and snow and ice management company in North America. He then served as president of Snow Management Group, which, among other large contracts, oversaw all snow and ice management operations for the 2002 Winter Olympics in Salt Lake City, Utah. He founded SIMA and served as its president for six years. He also served as a member of the ASCA's Industry Standards Committee, meaning he actually cowrote the first set of industry standards for the professional snow and ice management industry. He still serves on the ASCA's industry standards committee today. He's also the author of the industry's leading book on snow and ice practices for professionals, *Managing Snow and Ice* (first and second editions, 2011) as well as *Snow Management: A Look Through Time* (2016). In short, John wrote the book on the snow and ice management industry in more ways than one.

According to John, when the ASCA formed in 2010, one of the initial agreements among the members was that the industry lacked a set of written standards. There were, and still are, generally accepted practices, but at the time nothing was written down to help guide the contractor and property manager as to what was considered a best practice or a generally accepted practice.

From a legal perspective, there were only generally accepted practices to go on when trying to determine who was at fault from a liability standpoint in any kind of a slip-and-fall situation. Property managers were guessing at what they wanted, and contractors were guessing at what they were supplying. No one knew for sure what could be considered a best practice and what could not. After the formation of ASCA, a committee of ten people, including John, was assembled to flesh out what was to be considered these best practices and then write them down and publish them as a set of standards. The ASCA did that, and in 2011, it published the first iteration of the current standards.

But like most things, enacting a set of industry-wide standards wouldn't be that simple. "There was an individual who made an awful lot of noise, out of Florida, about the fact that these were just ten people's opinion as to what constituted best practice, and that there was nothing authoritative about them," John recalls. "They were not peer reviewed, as there was no recognized authority that recognized the standards as they were written."

In an attempt to rectify this complaint, the ASCA applied to the American National Accreditation Board (ANAB), asking to be recognized as a standards writing body, an application that ANAB would eventually approve. About a year later, John and his other nine cowriters submitted the standards they had written for peer review and recognition to ANSI. Approval from the ANSI took roughly a year and a half, before the final iteration of industry standards was completed and sent out to additional peer reviewers, property managers, attorneys, insurance agencies, and snow contractors.

"They had several months in order to review the standards as they were written and then ask questions or provide feedback or recommend changes," says John. "Every one of those who submitted any kind of a question or recommendation, every one of those was reviewed by the ten-person committee, and we provided an answer, saying, 'Yes, this is a good idea,' or 'No, and this is why.' It's a fairly lengthy process."

In February 2014, the finished and ANSI-recognized industry standards were finally published and distributed through ANSI. To add more credibility to them, John and his fellow ASCA committee members sent the industry standards to the ISO.

The ASCA simply wanted to gain ISO certification for snow contractors as a means to add one more level of credibility to what they do. If a contractor is ISO certified, then people buying snow services know (as long as they are educated on the meaning of these certifications, of course) that the contractor has a process that is written down, repeatable, measurable, and that they can put their finger on the different methods they're using to find out what's working and what's not. They should also know that if they have any kind of a problem, then the contractor will conduct a management review every year to adjust their procedures and become a better, more well-rounded company.

The ISO certification body also needs to be approved by the ANAB, as an entity that comes into a company, such as Invictus, and goes through their processes to make sure that they follow the *ANSI/ASCA A1000-2014.* That standards list is the basis for the ISO certification. A contractor must be performing to those standards, as well as the ISO 9001 SN standards for the snow and ice management industry, to receive certification from the ISO. None of this is law, but it is recognized internationally as a certification that means you're abiding by ISO standards as well as the ANSI standards, and that is helpful toward contractors attaining quality insurance, gaining customers, and insulating themselves from lawsuits.

DISCONNECTED: BUILDING A NETWORK, CREATING SPECIALISTS

Snow and ice management from the mid-1990s into the early 2000s was a very profitable business, but that was largely because there wasn't a lot of competition. A few things changed the industry around that time. The equipment that was available to those who plowed snow was unsophisticated and very limited because so few people manufactured it. There was also no information available to people who plowed snow about how to become better at accounting or sales or how to be a better businessperson in general. There wasn't a lot of attention paid to what was going on in the industry by the attorneys either. The industry was small, detached, and largely ignored by everyone outside the niche.

But if you look at what was going on in the mid-1990s, you see that large shopping malls were more prevalent and better frequented by the public during that era. All of the large snowplowing, meaning big malls and plazas, was handled mostly by construction contractors with heavy equipment. It wasn't being done by landscapers because they didn't have the right equipment. Those malls were plowed by the hour by contractors with Cat 960s and other pieces of heavy equipment. Plows for the fronts of loaders weren't readily available yet, and snow pushers were unheard of at the time. What was out there was being made in backyards and personal garages, usually from oil tanks cut in half. To make matters worse, there was no way to get educational information to people in the snow business. There were no trade magazines, no websites, no books. Nothing.

John decided to start SIMA in the mid-1990s to improve upon these issues. "The year after SIMA was born, the first symposium was held in Pittsburgh, where it was essentially the first gathering of only snow people to talk about how they do business," John explains. "The first year, there were well under a hundred people, more like sixty or seventy. The next year, there were a hundred and fifty, and the year after that, there were three hundred." As the industry got more organized, it began to explode with growth.

INDUSTRY GAME CHANGER

"The year after SIMA was born, the first symposium was held in Pittsburgh, where it was essentially the first gathering of only snow people to talk about how they do business," John explains. "The first year, there were well under a hundred people, more like sixty or seventy. The next year, there were a hundred and fifty, and the year after that, there were three hundred." As the industry got more organized, it began to explode with growth.

Two years after SIMA was born, the association began publishing the first magazine dedicated to the industry, *Snow Business* (after it was published for a short time under the name *Snow and Ice Manager* by *Landscape Management Magazine*). The magazine allowed advertising, and it wasn't long before people were getting the word out that they had equipment that would be useful to the industry.

With an avenue for inventors to get their creations into the marketplace, the industry began to innovate its tactics and evolve at a rapid rate, growing in size and sophistication year after year. This newfound network is how snow pushers came to be so widely used. Before, they were knockoffs, and John says that most people built them with small buzz box welders in the same mechanic room where they serviced their trucks.

With more efficient equipment, snowfighters began figuring out how to manage snow on large tracts of pavement. Suddenly, more contractors were making money from snow and ice, and magazine advertising revenues went up so much that a second magazine popped up in 2010. Before long, a contractor in Kansas City operating 350 pieces of snow equipment realized that he couldn't keep track of what his employees were doing, so he hired a software engineer to develop the first tracking program for snowfighters. The program eventually became CrewTracker, a tool that allows contractors to keep track of the time a crew is on each site as well as air and surface temperatures and other features.

"All of this sophistication came about as a result of the magazines, because now we were getting education to all kinds of people who were plowing snow," says John. "Then, the snowplowers themselves were saying, 'Well, geez, I've got a piece of equipment that's fabulous. I can make this work.'"

There was a downside, however, to all of this growth and added sophistication in the way of equipment and standards. Lawyers started to get involved because they recognized the financial opportunities posed by a growing, increasingly organized industry responsible for public safety and with so much liability. "We can make some money on this," I imagine they might have said. "Somebody slipped and fell and hurt themselves. They're not keeping the place safe. There are two organizations telling them how to keep things safe, and these guys aren't doing it, so let's start suing."

The lawsuits led the property owners and managers to push more liability off onto the snow contractor, which in turn led the snow contractor's insurance company to raise their rates due to their high litigation risk. And now, here we are, at a time when insurance companies and snow contractors are trying to work together to make the industry safer from lawsuits for the sake of both their businesses.

QUALITY TIME: THE MARK OF A SPECIALIST

It takes approximately sixty days for us to prepare an average site for a winter event. That figure jumps out as a surprise for a lot of clients, and I admit that I myself would have raised an eyebrow over the number before I got into the business. But, as is the way of most things, doing something right takes time. From the time we write the agreement with the customer to the time that we do a presite inspection, get the customer to sign off on any damages (or attest to no damage), and get our guys oriented with the site, two months might have passed. That takes a lot of planning and patience from both parties involved, us and the customer. When we talk to customers, we let them know that by August 31, we would like to have all our clients in the door and ready to go. Ideally, we won't take any more business after August 31. If you called us in September or October, if we had done our homework and already had the majority of our business locked down for the season, we might have to tell you that we'd love to work with you next year and wish you luck on the upcoming winter season. When you take a site because you really need the business, you compromise your standards by not giving yourself enough time to prepare and do the job properly. We moved away from that as soon as we could, and I certainly don't miss the stress that it caused.

Property owners and managers are also in a tough spot, considering how many responsibilities they have to a site. "Property managers know a little about a lot of things, but they don't know a lot about anything," says John. "They're being tasked by property owners with lowering costs, but what the property owners should be saying is, 'I want the lowest *responsible* price for acceptable quality service.' They leave out that last part, and the property manager says, 'Oh, I got to beat them up to get the lowest possible price.' The only place, oftentimes, that the contractor can shortcut something is in the quality of the work to achieve the desired pricing. It is the intelligent and educated property manager that thinks quality first and pricing third or fourth down the list. It is out there because a number of years ago, SIMA did a survey of property managers throughout North America, asking what it is they seek when they look for a snow contractor to outsource the work to, and price was number four on the list. Length of service, reputation, and the ability to provide a safe environment were the first three."

Most of our customers are large property owners of sites such as malls, industrial sites, big box retailers, and the like. We try our hardest to work with only clients who understand the importance of getting the job done right. We are having much more success operating in that realm of clientele than we were when we first started, and it's mostly because those types of clients prioritize ISO standards and safety. They get the fact that there will be fifteen to twenty pieces of equipment on their site to make it nice and safe, and as long as it's made nice and safe, they don't have a problem with that. The time it takes to do a job can't be measured by any real exact formula. We can't estimate how many minutes it will take a crew of two to clean a site measuring X number of square feet, because we don't have an exact way of knowing what the weather will be, what type of snow and ice the crew might encounter, or how many cars or other obstructions will be present. We can come up with a guesstimate that gets fairly close, but the conditions for each site are different every time we plow.

We can tell our clients how much certain services will cost, and because snow and ice management equipment, wages, and insurance expenses are so high, the price point is not cheap. Like most specialists, we prefer clients who understand those costs and why they are necessary. At the end of the day, this is a service that must be done, and to ensure people's safety, it must be done carefully, competently, and often.

We don't get heavy amounts of snowfall around Vancouver like they do around the Great Lakes or in other parts of Canada and the United States. We are risk managing sites for slip and falls, primarily, by battling against frozen ground. In our region, fog often rolls in off the ocean, or you might be in a low-lying area where, because the air temperature and the ground temperature differ so greatly, the ground freezes. It could also rain one night and freeze, and then we have a mass of black ice on the site that is very dangerous and must be dealt with immediately.

For the customers who don't get that or who don't want to or simply can't pay for proper preparation and maintenance, quite frankly, I can't take them on as customers. The customers who have managed the risks before and understand the seriousness they present, they understand our position and the costs associated with it, that they are fully invested in prioritizing a good service. If they're a trucking outfit, for example, they know they can't move their trucks when there is black ice all over the place. They have seen it before. They deal with it all the time, and they know it will cost them more in lost business and accidents than it will to pay us to take care of it. The property manager working in an office overseeing fifteen to twenty small properties miles away is usually just worried about the bottom line for their customer. Unfortunately, they don't typically see the bigger picture when they see an estimate for costs, and for them, the figure can be a shock. It's not uncommon for large sites to pay $300,000 or more for salting every season, but considering the loss they could suffer from lack of business or lawsuits, it's worth it to them.

In the past, like many snow and ice management upstarts, I would take a bad deal and try to make up my costs somewhere in the billing. If the property owner or manager told me I couldn't plow unless there was three or more inches of snow on the ground, I would go out and service a zero- to two-inch snowfall anyway because I know the risks involved even with that small amount of snow. When you're the one liable for the risks, you want to cover yourself as much as possible, so you just do the service for free.

But as we grew and gained more experienced, I realized the pains we go through on the invoicing side and on the back end. It is just too painful to even accept contract terms that dictate the triggers for when we can service and how much anymore. Ten years ago I could probably get away with just pushing them through without much of a problem. An hour here, an hour there—it wouldn't be that big of a deal. It was commonly accepted by my colleagues too, but now with technology the way it is and the way we are asking for to-the-minute reporting, there's just no room for that type of leeway. Having been burned a couple of times as well, I have zero tolerance for taking that type of risk today. A lot of other contractors will still take that risk, however, some even with a smile on their face, either from lack of experience, desperation, or both. For Invictus, turning down contracts that gave us very little control over how we serviced a site helped us avoid potentially bankruptcy-inducing legal fights, overextended payrolls, and neglected clients due to the obligation of catering to incompetent contract terms. To business owners, particularly those new to the industry, it may seem counterproductive to turn down tens of thousands of dollars from a potential client. And in the short term, it is. But saying no to bad contracts gives you the freedom to operate in the best ways possible according to your given area. As a result, you have more control over your reputation, meaning long-term growth and stronger customer loyalty. The revenue increase that eventually comes from that decision is obviously great, but the peace of mind in being able to freely decide how to service sites and protect your business is priceless.

INDUSTRY GAME CHANGER:

For Invictus, turning down contracts that gave us very little control over how we serviced a site helped us avoid potentially bankruptcy-inducing legal fights, overextended payrolls, and neglected clients due to the obligation of catering to incompetent contract terms. To business owners, particularly those new to the industry, it may seem counter-productive to turn down tens of thousands of dollars from a potential client. And in the short term, it is. But saying no to bad contracts gives you the freedom to operate in the best ways possible according to your given area. As a result, you have more control over your reputation, meaning long-term growth and stronger customer loyalty. The revenue increase that eventually comes from that decision is obviously great, but the peace of mind in being able to freely decide how to service sites and protect your business is priceless.

There has also been a history of property managers allowing contractors to have a very large carrot dangled in front of them in the way they price their services. If a contractor is servicing a property by the hour or by the ton, that contractor is going to be tempted to make up for any shortfalls in revenue by playing with the bills because it is just so easy. In the middle of the night, the property manager who is paying an hourly rate has no idea how many pieces of equipment the contractor has on site or how many hours a crew was there. See the problem?

From the customer's perspective, that uncertainty is a big driver behind much of the more recent interest in snow and ice management technology. Because we can access so much information about virtually anything we want, people are expecting to have more information on their sites. As evidenced by our adoption of new technology systems, that phenomenon hasn't missed our business, and the superior organization it offers is good for both us and our clients. It allows us to better gauge what our costs will be, so we can set flat rates rather than rates based on hours and tonnage. We can remain profitable, the property owner or property manager can create a firmer budget plan, and there's much less stress on both ends because we don't have to haggle quite as much over billing during the season.

In recent years, it's become more common for developers to design systems specific to the needs of the snow and ice management industry. As a result, it's even more common to see snow and ice companies integrating more technology into their services. In fact, companies spent hundreds of thousands of dollars building their own software and their own apps to the point that now, for as little as two dollars per site, I can monitor all my sites and receive notifications when there is a problem or when a service is needed. We can pass that technology, and the transparency that comes along with it, on to the customer. That has become a major driver for improving our communications with customers and educating them on our industry.

As a customer, you have to make sure that the specialist in question has two things in particular: (1) standards, and (2) assurance that you know what those standards are (these give you an idea of how they are going to operate). But it's also important to note whether they're using technology to manage the site. The use of technology to manage a site should be a given today, as more and more clients are requesting that side of it. For the best quality in a professional, make sure they have standards for their operations and that they are using technology that allows you to know exactly what's going on with your site. There shouldn't be any reason for a specialist not to meet these requirements, because standards and tech-based monitoring tools are really the best ways for them to manage their sites and cover themselves from any potential lawsuits.

> **The use of technology to manage a site should be a given today, as more and more clients are requesting that side of it.**

Things are changing in the industry. You can trace those changes back to a rise in successful slip-and-fall litigation. You can trace them back to the insurance providers not insuring properly. You can trace that development even further back to service providers not doing a high-quality job, which in most cases can be traced back to the property owner either not hiring a qualified professional or not allowing the professional they hired to do their job correctly.

The first thing a customer can do when hiring a snowfighter is to ensure that they are insured for snow and ice. That's a good indicator that they are fully dedicated to snow and ice management and able to consistently execute quality standards, given the nature of today's snow and ice insurance climate. A few companies are beginning to get on the ball with standardizing their processes and focusing solely on snow and ice management, and those are the guys you want to use. Strange as it may seem, I actually want to encourage other companies to do what we are doing at Invictus, so that our voice becomes louder. Hence, one of the reasons why I'm writing this book.

The results of the ASCA's work should inspire us all to push for a better industry. Illinois and Colorado, for example, now have legal documentation around hold harmless agreements for the snow and ice management business. That means that a property owner cannot be held harmless in a suit, if the contractor did everything to standard and the job was done right. If there's a slip-and-fall lawsuit, but the contractor performed to the best of their ability, everything was documented, and it was signed off on by the company that hired the contractor, then liability for the accident cannot fall completely on the contractor anymore. Now the liability falls partly on the owner of the property and their insurances, which in turn helps keep the insurance for the snowfighter down and thus lowers the annual costs for the property owner.

I see these changes as a win-win for the industry and the customer. Cleaning up the business and making it fair is a worthwhile legacy for me and my business, and that's what I want to see happen. I might as well. After all, if you're going to do something, you might as well do it all the way. It's the only way to be great. When I was running Invictus as a janitorial, landscaping, and snow and ice management company, I could never get the message clear because we were doing so many different things. But now that we are doing only one thing, we can do it the best that we possibly can. We can really focus on what we are passionate about in our work as well as what we stand for as an organization. That, to me, is what a specialist truly is, and whether you're a customer or a snowfighter, it's that passion, competency, and singular focus that you should look for first when scouting out a snow and ice management company of your own.

That also serves in your favor on the insurance side of the issue. Underwriters are beginning to understand that there is a sophistication that comes with these industry standards, having observed that the long-term effect of abiding by industry standards is that claims activity comes down. The insurance industry is becoming more and more educated about our business and the importance of hiring a specialist, and that's very good for certified snowfighters and property owners alike.

CHAPTER ELEVEN
THE INVICTUS WAY

It took roughly fourteen years running my business before I felt comfortable stepping away from my team. For years, I felt sheer panic rising in me when I was away from the office for any length of time. Taking a day or two off still included me checking my phone every few minutes or calling in to ask how things were going every few hours. A trip was usually business related, and a vacation without cell service was out of the question. And while it may have been necessary in those early years, I knew that it was unreasonable and completely unsustainable. The problem was that I didn't know how to get on top of the problem. I felt as though I was running on a giant ball, and if I slowed down or let something break my concentration, even for a moment, everything would come crashing down. Like I said, it was unreasonable, and I knew I couldn't go on like that forever—maybe not even another week.

Stepping away from your business, even if it's just a step or two, and trusting that the whole thing won't go off the rails is difficult for every business owner. You want to make sure that things are done right, so you do it yourself, which is to say that you end up doing pretty much everything. When most people start their own small business, they're doing everything from the deliverables to customer support to collecting payments to cleaning the bathroom. I was no different, and for many years I worked *in* my business more than I worked *on* it.

To get to the point that I understood what it meant to work on the business took time. It wasn't until seven or eight years ago when I joined a group called the Entrepreneur's Organization (EO) that I began to see how more efficient, effective, and, honestly, how much better for everyone it would be if I was the leader of the company rather than just the head worker in the business. Most of those teachings came to me by learning how my peers ran their businesses as well as enrolling in several business classes and workshops. Despite all the valuable lessons I learned from those sources, I realized that there is no school or organization out there that can give you hands-on teachings that are specific to your business. There are certainly courses you can take and groups like the EO that you can join and involve yourself with, but every business is just a little bit different, because every person is a little bit different. That means that learning how to work on your business is going to be a fairly personal process in the end. Work hard to learn as much as you can from others, but understand that at the end of the day, it's up to you to try new things and figure out what works, what doesn't, and why. As they say, you have to learn all the rules before you know which ones to break and when.

I feel that I've gotten much better at trusting myself and those around me, but it certainly took time. Being a business leader comes

> I began to see how more efficient, effective, and, honestly, how much better for everyone it would be if I was the leader of the company rather than just the head worker in the business.

more naturally to some than it does to others, but if you keep at it, it will come to you no matter how much you might doubt yourself at times.

LESSONS IN LEADERSHIP

One of the biggest assets in my struggle to become a better leader came when I learned how to hire better. If I could bring in better people, I realized, then I could focus on the big-picture items without worrying so much about whether the day-to-day responsibilities would get done. That doesn't mean that I always get my hires right. I'm learning constantly what a professional is and how they should perform.

When I think about being a professional company, however, I want to emulate the great sports teams out there. I think about how they operate, how they recruit, how they train, and how they use their players. Typically, the best teams find highly qualified players that are excellent gifted specimens. We can find those people to work in our businesses too. On different levels, obviously, but they're out there.

That's the main difference that I've had to adjust to in the shift from worker to leader: thinking about improvements to the company and the entire industry itself, rather than thinking about what needs to get done in the here and now. The majority of my time today I spend working on the vision and culture of the organization.

The option to run two different outfits from one location wouldn't have been possible had we not formulated a set of services that every team member learns through a series of training sessions. The key for us was to identify what our clients wanted, what we wanted, and how much it would cost to keep everyone happy.

Client needs, company needs, and an agreeable price point—with those three things in place, you can write the playbook that keeps it all running smoothly and allow yourself the space to configure the process as needed and plan for the future.

CHOOSE YOUR COVERAGE

Over the years, we saw that many clients were struggling to decide what kind of coverage best suited their sites. You really can't predict the weather, at least not with 100 percent accuracy and certainly not a year or even a quarter in advance. That's a problem for both snow and ice contractors and property owners and managers. To make matters worse, few property owners and managers have expert knowledge on the ins and outs of snow and ice management, making the complicated decisions of when and how their properties should be cared for that much more difficult.

Hoping to make our clients' choices easier, Invictus opted to offer them two service packages. Of course, that move didn't settle into play until after we made several changes to each plan, even cutting a few services and packages from the lineup. The idea was that since we know exactly how to respond to nearly every winter weather event in our area, we should be able to consolidate our strategies and techniques into a few battle plans, so to speak, and then determine what our costs for each plan would be, accounting for man power, materials, average number of hours, and so on. We also had to stay mindful of fluctuating operating expenses, such as fuel, salt, wages, taxes, insurance, various inflation costs, and more. The other motivating factor for creating simple package plans was to make it easier for our clients to budget the services they receive from us. With a seasonal package billed at a flat rate, a property owner or manager knows exactly how much money they will need to set aside each year, quarter, or month.

LEARNING THE CULTURE ROPES

Culture is a term that gets thrown around a lot these days. I will tell you this: creating a functional, healthy culture that enhances your company is far easier said than done. It requires equal amounts of intention and dedication, which means you really need to be all in on the concept of culture and its benefits for the process of developing your own to be successful. It's a lot of work, and it demands a fair amount of reflection with a somewhat philosophical eye to discover what your culture is and what you want it to be. But what is culture exactly?

There are many ways to define it, and honestly, there are better experts than me on the subject, but I'll give you my take on it based on what I've learned through lectures, workshops, and reading material over the years. Company culture is about the journey to understand *why* you and your company exist (purpose). Knowing your purpose is the first step, and for us, that was fairly easy: we exist to keep people safe and from being inconvenienced by snow and ice. That was pretty simple for us, but the other side of it is the idea of *how* you should behave (core values) to support your purpose, in ways that are more philosophical than practical. The answers to these questions form the ideology of a company, defining the backbone of what inspires and directs its business strategies, managerial style, and marketing tactics as well as its products and services. That ideology should also guide what *not* to do just as much as it guides what to do. Rejecting the wrong ideas is just as important, if not more important, than saying yes to the right ones. And your core ideology as a company—your sense of purpose and values—is what directs those tough decisions, especially when the answer is not clear.

Every company has a culture. Whether it's an intentionally designed culture or one that just exists through a lack of doing anything about it is up to the leadership. The cultures that exist by default are certainly the easiest cultures to have, but that doesn't mean that they're good ones. They aren't the kind that hold up under pressure, nor are they the type that sustain themselves and inform the company's purpose. And a company without a clear purpose—that is, a simple, well-defined, and sincere reason for being—is a company that invariably struggles to inspire its team to work with a sense of purpose.

For Invictus, we need to have a competitive nature to ourselves and our team because we get pressed really hard during a strong weather event. We are a performance culture, built around the action of our dangerous and labor-intensive work. But outside of that, we have a laid-back culture. We stress that we want to be extremely professional and do things the best way possible within our marketplace, but the actual difference between how we perform in the fall and winter compared to how we are in the spring and summer may seem quite extreme.

I don't let everyone come to work in shorts and flip-flops in the summer, mind you. We still have regular contact with our customers and contractors, and we want to present a branded look all the time, but things are more relaxed because we are not responding to weather events and trying to deploy crews around the clock. We are in the process of creating a culture inside the office and among our contractors that promotes the snow and ice industry. We are doing that by finding ways to inform the public about the technical aspects of what we do as well as making it fun and accessible.

One strategy for marrying these two culture goals has been our annual golf tournament. Last year we had roughly 145 people there, a mix of contractors, industry colleagues, and customers. We don't always sponsor a hole at our own golf tournament, but we did last year, and we decided to have a couple of games set up there for our customers to enjoy. To get into the game, a would-be contestant had to read our "Did You Know," which included ISO standards, insurance statistics, and dates around when snow and ice management preparations need to get started in our area. Once they finished reading, they could play a game for a nice bottle of wine or liquor in a wooden crate. But before they could enter the game, they had to give us their "winter name." When people asked us what a winter name was, we explained that we recently began giving ourselves nicknames in the theme of winter for fun—names like "Snow Warrior," "Queen Blizzard," or "Iceman." It's a way to put everyone into the snow and ice mood, so to speak, and everyone had a good laugh thinking of their winter nicknames and listening to what the others had chosen.

Another team-building event we've recently put into play is our annual end-of-the-season "Snowfighters Games," during which our entire staff is divided into multiple teams and competes for prizes based on the speed and quality with which they complete a number of events. The events include shoveling snow, spreading salt, maneuvering plow trucks through obstacles, and more. We've had great success with it so far, and though it's currently only Invictus contractors and subcontractors participating, my goal is to one day turn it into a gathering where all North American snow and ice management companies can come together, compete for fun, and exchange ideas.

Culturally, we are trying to balance safety and fun. The ISO part of it is an intentional piece of our safety culture, where we want to have a really safe environment for everyone to work. We want our customers and team members alike to understand what thoroughness looks like, and that comes through the processes of preparing for the winter (i.e., maintaining equipment, deciding on deicing and anti-icing methods, plotting routes, communicating with local government agencies to locate gaps in service areas, assessing your insurance coverage, finalizing service terms and packages, and budgeting expenses).

The other side of our culture plan is to strengthen the learning and core values aspects of the company. We now use those priorities as a lens for nearly everything we do. I coach my team through that lens. We hire through that lens. We recruit and service our customers through that lens. We ripped the lens apart to make sure it was the right one, using our core values as our guide.

The uncertainty of all the changes in today's world makes it tempting to dismiss the warning signs that companies need to update their strategies. It urges us either to keep doing what's familiar because it *kind of* works or to become paralyzed by the overwhelming thought of how much we may have to change. Old habits die hard, as they say. Like it or not, though, change is happening everywhere, every day, to everyone, and if you don't lay down a strong foundation (i.e., your company culture), adjusting to that change only becomes more difficult than it already is.

Experimentation is required to drive change, because it forces you out of your comfort zone and into your growth zone. It forces you to try things that are different from what you have done before and to examine the incremental change. But before anyone can feel comfortable taking risks and experimenting with ideas, they have to know that it's safe for them to fail. This demands an organization to prioritize strategies meant to cultivate vulnerability in their staff and members, because an experimentation culture without vulnerability doesn't lead to true introspection and learning.

Building such a culture must start from the top. To expect people throughout an organization to show their vulnerability when the top leaders are infallible is unrealistic. Most top leaders claim they are open to feedback, but when they actually receive critical feedback, they rarely listen actively and take the input into consideration.

In an environment in which people feel comfortable talking about their failures and showing their vulnerability to risk, a feedback loop opens up that makes experimentation useful. If you're not willing to be vulnerable and encourage others to experiment, then people are going to search for theoretical success rather than trying to figure out what's actually happening. The trick is that when you fail, you fail in the pursuit of something good, and you fail differently than how you might have failed before. All that's important is that people learn from failure and share that knowledge with others. The hope is that the next time they or their colleagues fail, they don't fail the same way. You don't want to encourage failure the same way over and over, nor do you want failure to be for lack of

The trick is that when you fail, you fail in the pursuit of something good, and you fail differently than how you might have failed before.

effort or insight. You want to encourage trying something new that advances your goals, and if it fails from time to time, that's not only OK but something you should consider a win. It's a win because you learned something new that makes you smarter, faster, and more agile.

Advances that have occurred throughout human history in fields as diverse as science, literature, art, and exploration have not taken place because folks were content with repeating the past. They sought to experiment, to seek new knowledge, and to find new and better ways forward. Today is no different. Associations are no different. To meaningfully advance, we must be willing to embrace failure as a way to learn and improve.

But a culture of experimentation needs fail-safes in place too, especially in a field like ours where people's lives and the safety of the public are at stake. A willingness to fail doesn't mean you throw all your crew into a snowstorm with a gadget you haven't tested and a new technique you've never tried and see if it works out OK. That's not the type of experimentation I'm talking about. I'm talking about experimenting in very small, incremental ways that allow you to test the waters before you dive in. Metaphorically speaking, you should first throw small rocks (low-cost, low-risk, low-distraction experiments) onto the ice (meaning your operational methods) to learn which ideas will support the work and which will break it. Then you can allocate more resources to the successful ideas. Extrapolating small, successful ideas (rocks) into huge boulders, so to speak, has a much greater impact than does innovation for the sake of innovating.

That kind of small-scale experimentation is incredibly important toward easing the company into a new culture, because you're able to learn from the experience on a dynamic level, rather than just sitting around theorizing about what may or may not happen. After all, to move through a dark room, it's better to take short, slow steps and learn from the bumps, especially if the alternatives are standing still or running.

CORE VALUES: KNOWING YOUR WORTH, KNOWING YOUR LIMITS

Core values are typically defined as a set of behaviors that a company agrees to hold itself to no matter what. They inform your decision-making at every level and ultimately shape the overall character of the company.

It's funny to me now that when I think back to six or seven years ago, I recall a time when we were operating with some dozen or more core values. That's a lot of rules to live by, and not only could I *not* remember them all; no one else ever could either. After a few years, we decided to make life a little easier on ourselves and pare them down to four. But, as you might imagine, it's actually more difficult to define yourself by fewer values than it is to give yourself more.

To me, the core values don't mean much unless you actually live them. Like your purpose, your values already exist; you just need to choose which ones are most important to you and which ones are most relevant to the company as a whole.

I believe that values are already ingrained into people. Whether through their parents, their schooling, their childhood environment, or other experiences and influences they encountered early on in their lives, individual values already exist, but over time they may become hazy, at best.

Every individual has baked into them their own personal core values, which set the standard for their behavior and form a custom vision for what they see as important in life. There are, of course, certain values that just about everyone agrees with, and to one degree or another, aspires to implement in their lives. Things like honesty, work ethic, trustworthiness, and integrity are all values that most people look up to, but they aren't necessarily the kind that make a company unique. After all, who wants to do business with anyone who doesn't believe in these values? They are, more or less, a given in any industry, the kind of values that are assumed rather than promoted.

While everyone has a specific set of values "coded" into them, they are rarely asked to identify them. That's the struggle in "discovering" your values as an individual or as a company. Creating a set of values that uniquely define what is different and compelling about your organization often varies, depending on who you ask. When you do try to identify your company's core values, oftentimes rarely discussed values will suddenly come into glaring focus as personalities either clash or gel. The effect can be both intimidating and unifying, but everyone should be heard and have his or her values considered, without exception. For me, the easiest way to settle on a set of collective core values is to find the values that are the most interesting, authentic, effective, and majority approved.

Discovering your values is, unfortunately, just the beginning. I've heard it over and over again, that the hardest part is to take core values from a concept into an actual living thing within the company. It takes time; there's no doubt about it. We've had to revamp our core values a few times. I've even been in meetings when someone asks me what my core values are, and I couldn't remember them because I wasn't living them. How could I ever expect my employees to remember them, let alone live them, if I wasn't? The keys here are consistency and patience. With a constant talk around our values, our team eventually grew to not only remember them but to really understand and use them as well.

CONCLUSION

If there's one thing you take away from this book, let it be this: snowfighting is a critical-need service. It's vital to public safety and operations. Without us, next to nothing would function during times of snow and ice. Air and road travel, shipping, commerce, law enforcement, fire and medical crews, and much more all depend on snowfighters to keep things safe and moving. When the importance of our industry is fully realized and appreciated, the problems that lay before today will be much easier to solve. Property owners and managers, contractors and subcontractors, governments, insurance carriers, the legal system, and the general public alike—we all have a stake in this industry succeeding. As such, we all have a role to play in ensuring that it does as well.

Snow and ice management is more akin to emergency response services than it is to a trade. And while that fact is important for everyone to keep in mind, it should be of special importance for property owners and managers and snowfighters themselves. Snowfighters must be ready to respond to swift weather events and calls at all times. Unlike fire and rescue services, however, commercial snowfighters can't shut down a site to make it safe. They will often have to work around cars and people to complete their job. Raising the industry's standards through accreditation may help to maintain safer and more effective practices, leading to fewer accidents, better results, and a stronger reputation overall. Fewer accidents and a solid reputation for the entire industry would provide individual snow-fighters with a better position when negotiating legislation, insurance costs, and service contracts.

The introduction of ISO certification into the industry isn't just good for the contractor; it's good for the customer too. In case you've forgotten, the ISO is a standards organization with its origins stretching back to the post–World War II industrial boom. Today, being an ISO-certified company means you know and follow processes and procedures that are generally regarded as the global standard in a particular industry. Invictus received its ISO status through a program specifically tailored to the snow and ice industry (SN 9001), becoming the first snow and ice company in the Pacific Northwest to have such a certification. Organizations like the ISO help snow-fighters stay up to date on industry standards and best practices as well as offer property owners and managers an additional filter when choosing a contractor. It's a win-win solution to the issue of creating more industry-wide compliance and consistency.

Operating a snow and ice company is risky business. There's a lot at stake when your business requires operating regularly in unpredictable and dangerous conditions. For snowfighters, the margin for error is often as slim as the margin for profits, with one depending heavily on the other. The pressure of this industry has a tendency to weed people out quickly, which works in favor of the entrepreneur who is willing to take the risks and who is able to withstand the challenges that come with them. Take advantage of that fact by learning from the veterans. No one knows more about adapting to change and finding a path through the risks than those who have survived long enough to be successful.

It's also important to remember that the snow and ice management industry greatly expands and contracts annually, and it relies heavily on other trades. According to the ASCA, an estimated 35,000 snow and ice management companies operate in North America, employing more than 400,000 people every winter. The average company earns $542,000 in seasonal revenue and employs seven year-round, full-time workers; three year-round, part-time workers; twelve seasonal workers; and ten subcontracting companies. For its part, the average subcontractor employs between one and thirty workers, depending on the location and size of the market. Sixty-seven percent of snow contractors also run a landscaping business at least part of the year. Nearly all the rest operate in a related segment of the labor industry (e.g., excavating, general contracting, and road construction).

While companies dedicated fully to snow and ice management prepare and strategize year round, the bulk of the sweat work occurs in the winter months. That can be challenging with regard to keeping a crew together during the off-season. Ensuring that there is ample work, a solid work environment, and a good rate of pay is great, but companies also must find ways to engage their team members year round. Juggling that challenge is one reason you'll find the herd of year-round snow and ice management companies to be so thin, but it's far from the only one or even the primary one.

Due to the increase of slip-and-fall lawsuits, more and more snowfighters are refusing contracts that set service stipulations, such as when a site can be cleared, what materials can be used, or for how long a crew can be on the site. Because a lot of the snowfighter's work takes place at night, it's understandable that property owners and managers are often unsure of what exactly they're paying for. On the other hand, they may not want a crew in their parking lot during business hours. It's a double-edged sword for both parties. When property owners and managers afford more autonomy to the contractor, though, it allows them more options to devise a plan that services the site correctly, safely, and at minimal inconvenience to the property's function. Not only does that keep the risks down and the traffic moving; it also keeps the relationship between both groups from becoming unnecessarily strained.

Of course, for a property owner or manager to feel secure giving a contractor more control over service stipulations in their contract, they need to know that they're hiring someone who knows what they're doing and can be trusted to do the job well, even in the middle of the night with no one else around. To help ease those worries, property owners and managers should make sure to inquire about a contractor's certifications and company standards and procedures before hiring them.

Remember that both the property owner and the contractor can be liable for injuries on the site. Whether you're the contractor or the property owner, if a claim comes against your site, take immediate action to gather as much information as possible about the incident. Collect all the video footage, text messages, emails, paperwork, witness accounts, and anything else that may aid in your defense. The longer you wait, the harder it will be to obtain this information.

Let technology help you too. Unlike before, apps and tech gadgets designed specifically for the snow and ice world are on the rise. Integrating these tools into your business may take some time, but whether you're a property owner or manager or a contractor, the apps and gadgets will help you devise and keep track of service schedules, capture and store documentation, organize expenses, plan routes, and a host of other useful functions.

It may not sound like it, but distributing liability more fairly is actually good for everyone. Contracts that excuse property owners of liability and dictate when a contractor can service a site create a public safety concern. Fortunately, faced with the problem that such laws and practices are both bad for business and a threat to public safety, a wave of support for changes by lawmakers and property owners alike has begun to make its way into the industry in recent years. With these concerns finally being heard at congressional meetings, the doors of communication in government and the private sector have been opened, spurring more discussions between snowfighters, insurance companies, and property owners around how these problems can be resolved.

Above all, perhaps, is the need to narrow the knowledge gap between property managers and snow and ice contractors. That was, and is, a primary purpose behind my writing this book, and it should be a central focus of your individual business relationship as well. The more a property manager knows about a snowfighter's job and vice versa, the more service problems arising from misunderstandings drop dramatically. Contractors can create and offer their clients pamphlets or even courses aimed at teaching them some of the basics about what snow and ice management entails, including the types of equipment and techniques they use, region-specific weather conditions and how they affect the work, and a general overview of operating procedures so property managers have a better understanding of what they can expect from their service. Likewise, it's just as important for the contractor to have a basic understanding of a property manager's responsibilities as well as a thorough understanding of their snow and ice related concerns and expectations. Doing so helps providers design a service plan that meets the needs and interests of the property manager and owner while also setting realistic expectations and protections.

I believe we can do better. This industry can be more profitable, safer, more advanced, and ultimately more adaptable to myriad inevitable changes and challenges existing both now and in the future. But we have to do it together, as an entire network of individuals affected by the industry's work. It is not just a set of issues that contractors must figure out on their own, nor is it even possible for them to. It is possible, however, if we connect, communicate, and work on them together. It's the only way to keep everything that snow and ice reaches moving along uninterrupted. More importantly, it's how we keep everyone whom snow and ice touches safe.